# LOCOMOTIVES

FIFT

G000016243

The complete guide to all
Locomotives which operate on
the national railway
and Eurotunnel networks

Robert Pritchard & Peter Hall

ISBN 978 1909 431 19 5

© 2015. Platform 5 Publishing Ltd, 52 Broadfield Road, Sheffield, S8 0XJ, England.

Printed in England by The Lavenham Press, Lavenham, Suffolk.

# CONTENTS

# PROVISION OF INFORMATION

This book has been compiled with care to be as accurate as possible, but in some cases information is not easily available and the publisher cannot be held responsible for any errors or omissions. We would like to thank the companies and individuals who have been co-operative in supplying information to us. The authors of this series of books are always pleased to receive notification from readers of any inaccuracies readers may find, to enhance future editions. Please send comments to:

Robert Pritchard, Platform 5 Publishing Ltd, 52 Broadfield Road, Sheffield, S8 0XJ, England.                **e-mail**: robert.pritchard@platform5.com

**Tel**: 0114 255 2625      **Fax**: 0114 255 2471.

This book is updated to information received by 5 October 2015.

# UPDATES

This book is updated to the Stock Changes given in **Today's Railways UK 167** (November 2015). Readers are therefore advised to update this book from the official Platform 5 Stock Changes published every month in **Today's Railways UK** magazine, starting with issue 168.

The Platform 5 magazine Today's Railways UK contains news and rolling stock information on the railways of Great Britain and Ireland and is published on the second Monday of every month. For further details of Today's Railways UK, please see the advertisement on the back cover of this book.

---

**Front cover photograph:** New DRS-liveried 37423 leaves Millom with the 11.38 Barrow-in-Furness–Carlisle Northern service on 11/08/15.                **Tom McAtee**

# BRITAIN'S RAILWAY SYSTEM

## INFRASTRUCTURE & OPERATION

Britain's national railway infrastructure is owned by a "not for dividend" company, Network Rail. In September 2014 Network Rail was classified a public sector company, being described by the Government as a "public sector arm's-length body of the Department for Transport".

Many stations and maintenance depots are leased to and operated by Train Operating Companies (TOCs), but some larger stations are under Network Rail control. The only exception is the infrastructure on the Isle of Wight: Island Line was the only franchise that included the maintenance of the infrastructure as well as the operation of passenger services. As Island Line is now part of the South West Trains franchise, both the infrastructure and trains are operated by South West Trains.

Trains are operated by TOCs over Network Rail, regulated by access agreements between the parties involved. In general, TOCs are responsible for the provision and maintenance of the locomotives, rolling stock and staff necessary for the direct operation of services, whilst Network Rail is responsible for the provision and maintenance of the infrastructure and also for staff to regulate the operation of services.

The Department for Transport is the franchising authority for the national network, with Transport Scotland overseeing the award of the ScotRail franchise. Railway Franchise holders (TOCs) can take commercial risks, although some franchises are known as "management contracts", where ticket revenues pass directly to the DfT. Concessions (such as London Overground) see the operator paid a fee to run the service, usually within tightly specified guidelines. Operators running a Concession would not normally take commercial risks, although there are usually penalties and rewards in the contract.

During 2012 the letting of new franchises was suspended pending a review of the franchise system. The process was restarted in 2013 but it is taking a number of years to catch-up and several franchises are receiving short-term extensions (or "Direct Awards") in the meantime.

## DOMESTIC PASSENGER TRAIN OPERATORS

The large majority of passenger trains are operated by the TOCs on fixed-term franchises or concessions. Franchise expiry dates are shown in the list of franchisees below:

| Franchise | Franchisee | Trading Name |
|---|---|---|
| **Caledonian Sleeper** | Serco<br>(until 31 March 2030) | **Caledonian Sleeper** |

*This new franchise started in April 2015 when the ScotRail and ScotRail Sleeper franchises were split. Abellio won the ScotRail franchise and Serco the Caledonian Sleeper franchise. Caledonian Sleeper operates four trains nightly between London Euston and Scotland using locomotives hired from GBRf or DB Schenker. New CAF rolling stock will be introduced from 2018.*

| **Chiltern** | Arriva (Deutsche Bahn) | **Chiltern Railways** |
| | (until 31 December 2021) | |

Chiltern Railways operates a frequent service between London Marylebone, Banbury and Birmingham Snow Hill, with some peak trains extending to Kidderminster. There are also regular services from Marylebone to Stratford-upon-Avon and to Aylesbury Vale Parkway via Amersham (along the London Underground Metropolitan Line). A new route to Oxford Parkway was added to the franchise in autumn 2015, and this line will be extended to Oxford in 2016. The fleet consists of DMUs of Classes 121 (used on the Princes Risborough–Aylesbury route), 165, 168 and 172 plus a number of loco-hauled rakes used on some of the Birmingham route trains, worked by Class 68s hired from DRS.

| **Cross-Country** | Arriva (Deutsche Bahn) | **CrossCountry** |
| | (until October 2016) | |

*Franchise extension to be negotiated to October 2019.*

CrossCountry operates a network of long distance services between Scotland, North-East England and Manchester to the South-West of England, Reading, Southampton, Bournemouth and Guildford, centred on Birmingham New Street. These trains are mainly formed of diesel Class 220/221 Voyagers, supplemented by a small number of HSTs on the NE–SW route. Inter-urban services also link Nottingham, Leicester and Stansted Airport with Birmingham and Cardiff. These use Class 170 DMUs.

| **Crossrail** | MTR | **Crossrail** |
| | (until 30 May 2023) | |

*There is an option to extend the concession by 2 years to May 2025.*

This is a new concession which started in May 2015. Initially Crossrail took over the Liverpool Street–Shenfield stopping service from Abellio Greater Anglia, using a fleet of Class 315 EMUs. New Class 345 EMUs will be introduced on this route from spring 2017 and then from 2018–19 Crossrail will operate through new tunnels beneath central London, from Shenfield and Abbey Wood in the east to Reading and Heathrow in the west.

| **East Midlands** | Stagecoach Group | **East Midlands Trains** |
| | (until 4 March 2018) | |

*There is an option to extend the franchise by 1 year to March 2019.*

EMT operates a mix of long distance high speed services on the Midland Main Line (MML), from London St Pancras to Sheffield (Leeds at peak times and some extensions to York/Scarborough) and Nottingham, and local and regional services ranging from the Norwich–Liverpool route to Nottingham–Skegness, Nottingham–Mansfield–Worksop, Nottingham–Matlock and Derby–Crewe. It also operates local services in Lincolnshire. Trains on the MML are worked by a fleet of Class 222 DMUs and nine HSTs, whilst the local and regional fleet consists of DMU Classes 153, 156 and 158.

| **Essex Thameside** | National Express Group | **c2c** |
| | (until 8 November 2029) | |

*There is an option to extend the franchise by seven reporting periods to May 2030.*

c2c operates an intensive, principally commuter, service from London Fenchurch Street to Southend and Shoeburyness via both Upminster and Tilbury. The fleet consists entirely of Class 357 EMUs. In 2014 c2c won the new 15-year franchise that promised to introduce 17 new 4-car EMUs from 2019.

### Greater Western
First Group
(until 1 April 2019)
**Great Western Railway**

*There is an option to extend the franchise by 1 year to April 2020.*

Great Western Railway (until September 2015 branded as First Great Western) operates long distance trains from London Paddington to South Wales, the West Country and Worcester and Hereford. In addition there are frequent trains along the Thames Valley corridor to Newbury/Bedwyn and Oxford, plus local and regional trains throughout the South-West including the Cornish, Devon and Thames Valley branches, the Reading–Gatwick North Downs line and Cardiff–Portsmouth Harbour and Bristol–Weymouth regional routes. A fleet of 53 HSTs is used on the long-distance trains, with DMUs of Classes 165 and 166 used on the North Downs and Thames Valley routes and Class 180s used alongside HSTs on the Cotswold Line to Worcester and Hereford. Classes 143, 150, 153 and 158 are used on local and regional trains in the South-West. A small fleet of four Class 57s is maintained to principally work the overnight "Cornish Riviera" Sleeper service between London and Penzance.

### Greater Anglia
Abellio (Netherlands Railways)
(until 19 October 2016)
**Abellio Greater Anglia**

Abellio Greater Anglia operates main line trains between London Liverpool Street, Ipswich and Norwich and local trains across Norfolk, Suffolk and parts of Cambridgeshire. It also runs local and commuter services into Liverpool Street from the Great Eastern (including Southend, Braintree and Clacton) and West Anglia (including Cambridge and Stansted Airport) routes. It operates a varied fleet of Class 90s with loco-hauled Mark 3 sets, DMUs of Classes 153, 156 and 170 and EMUs of Classes 317, 321, 360 and 379. A locomotive-hauled set, with Class 37s, is hired from DRS for use on some trains between Norwich and Great Yarmouth/Lowestoft.

### Integrated Kent
Govia (Go-Ahead/Keolis)
(until 24 June 2018)
**Southeastern**

Southeastern operates all services in the South-East London suburbs, the whole of Kent and part of Sussex, which are primarily commuter services to London. It also operates domestic high speed trains on HS1 from London St Pancras to Ashford, Ramsgate, Dover and Faversham with additional peak services on other routes. EMUs of Classes 375, 376, 465 and 466 are used, along with Class 395s on the High Speed trains.

### InterCity East Coast
Stagecoach/Virgin Trains
(until 31 March 2023)
**Virgin Trains East Coast**

*There is an option to extend the franchise by 1 year to March 2024.*

Virgin Trains East Coast operates frequent long distance trains on the East Coast Main Line between London King's Cross, Leeds, York, Newcastle and Edinburgh, with less frequent services to Bradford, Harrogate, Skipton, Hull, Lincoln, Glasgow, Aberdeen and Inverness. A mixed fleet of Class 91s and 30 Mark 4 sets, and 15 HST sets, are used on these trains.

### InterCity West Coast
Virgin Rail Group (Virgin/Stagecoach Group)
(until September 2017)
**Virgin Trains**

Virgin Trains operates long distance services along the West Coast Main Line from London Euston to Birmingham/Wolverhampton, Manchester, Liverpool and Glasgow using Class 390 Pendolino EMUs. It also operates Class 221 Voyagers on the Euston–Chester–Holyhead route, whilst a mixture of 221s and 390s are used on the Euston–Birmingham–Glasgow/Edinburgh route.

| **London Rail** | MTR/Arriva (Deutsche Bahn) | **London Overground** |
| | (until 12 November 2016) | |

*This is a Concession and is different from other rail franchises, as fares and service levels are set by Transport for London instead of by the DfT.*

London Overground operates services on the Richmond–Stratford North London Line and the Willesden Junction–Clapham Junction West London Line, plus the East London Line from Highbury & Islington to New Cross and New Cross Gate, with extensions to Clapham Jn (via Denmark Hill), Crystal Palace and West Croydon. It also runs services from London Euston to Watford Junction. All these use Class 378 EMUs whilst Class 172 DMUs are used on the Gospel Oak–Barking route. London Overground also took over the operation of some suburban services from London Liverpool Street in 2015 – to Chingford, Enfield Town and Cheshunt. These use Class 315 and 317 EMUs.

| **Merseyrail Electrics** | Serco/Abellio (Netherlands Railways) | **Merseyrail** |
| | (until 19 July 2028) | |

*Under the control of Merseytravel PTE instead of the DfT. Franchise reviewed every five years to fit in with the Merseyside Local Transport Plan.*

Merseyrail operates services between Liverpool and Southport, Ormskirk, Kirkby, Hunts Cross, New Brighton, West Kirby, Chester and Ellesmere Port, using Class 507 and 508 EMUs.

| **Northern Rail** | Serco/Abellio (Netherlands Railways) | **Northern** |
| | (until 1 April 2016) | |

Northern operates a range of inter-urban, commuter and rural services throughout the North of England, including those around the cities of Leeds, Manchester, Sheffield, Liverpool and Newcastle. The network extends from Chathill in the north to Nottingham in the south, and Cleethorpes in the east to St Bees in the west. Long distance services include Leeds–Carlisle, Middlesbrough–Carlisle and York–Blackpool North. The operator uses a large fleet of DMUs of Classes 142, 144, 150, 153, 155, 156 and 158 plus EMU Classes 319, 321, 322, 323 and 333.

| **ScotRail** | Abellio (Netherlands Railways) | **ScotRail** |
| | (until 31 March 2022) | |

*There is an option to extend the franchise by 3 years to March 2025.*

ScotRail provides almost all passenger services within Scotland and also trains from Glasgow to Carlisle via Dumfries, some of which extend to Newcastle (jointly operated with Northern). The company operates a large fleet of DMUs of Classes 156, 158 and 170 and EMU Classes 314, 318, 320, 334 and 380. Two loco-hauled rakes are also used on Fife Circle commuter trains, hauled by Class 68s hired from DRS.

| **South Western** | Stagecoach Group | **South West Trains** |
| | (until June 2017) | |

South West Trains operates trains from London Waterloo to destinations across the South and South-West including Woking, Basingstoke, Southampton, Portsmouth, Salisbury, Exeter, Reading and Weymouth as well as suburban services from Waterloo. SWT also runs services between Ryde and Shanklin on the Isle of Wight, using former London Underground 1938 stock (Class 483s). The rest of the fleet consists of DMU Classes 158 and 159 and EMU Classes 444, 450, 455, 456 and 458.

| **Thameslink & Great Northern** | Govia (Go-Ahead/Keolis) | **Govia Thameslink Railway** |
| | (until 19 September 2021) | |

*There is an option to extend the franchise by 2 years to September 2023.*

Govia operates this franchise, the largest in the UK, as a management contract. The former

Southern franchise was combined with Thameslink/Great Northern in 2015. GTR uses four brands within the franchise: "Thameslink" operates trains between Bedford and Brighton via central London and also on the Sutton and Wimbledon loops using Class 319, 377 and 387 EMUs. Some trains continue into Southeastern territory to Sevenoaks, Orpington and Ashford. "Great Northern" comprises services from London King's Cross and Moorgate to Welwyn Garden City, Hertford North, Peterborough, Cambridge and Kings Lynn using Class 313, 317, 321 and 365 EMUs. "Southern" operates predominantly commuter services between London, Surrey and Sussex, as well as services along the South Coast between Southampton, Brighton, Hastings and Ashford, and also the cross-London service linking South Croydon and Milton Keynes. It also operates metro services in South London. Class 171 DMUs are used on Brighton–Ashford and London Bridge–Uckfield services, whilst all other services are in the hands of Class 313, 377 and 455 EMUs. Finally the premium "Gatwick Express" operates non-stop trains between London Victoria and Gatwick Airport using Class 442 EMUs (to be replaced by Class 387s in 2016). Some trains extend to/from Brighton in the peaks.

| **Trans-Pennine Express** | First Group/Keolis (until 1 April 2016) | **TransPennine Express** |
|---|---|---|

TransPennine Express operates predominantly long distance inter-urban services linking major cities across the North of England, along with Edinburgh and Glasgow in Scotland. The main services are Manchester Airport/Manchester Piccadilly–Newcastle/Middlesbrough/ Hull plus Liverpool–Scarborough and Liverpool–Newcastle along the North Trans-Pennine route via Huddersfield, Leeds and York, and Manchester Airport–Cleethorpes along the South Trans-Pennine route via Sheffield. TPE also operates Manchester Airport–Blackpool/ Barrow/Windermere/Edinburgh/Glasgow. The fleet consists of DMU Classes 170 (used on the Cleethorpes routes, but to transfer to Chiltern Railways) and 185 and also new Class 350 EMUs used on Manchester Airport–Scotland services. To cover for the loss of Class 170s to Chiltern, Class 156s are being hired from Northern for use on some Manchester Airport–Blackpool North services.

| **Wales & Borders** | Arriva (Deutsche Bahn) (until 14 October 2018)* | **Arriva Trains Wales** |
|---|---|---|

*The franchise agreement includes the provision for the term to be further extended by mutual agreement by up to five years beyond October 2018. Management of the franchise is devolved to the Welsh Government, but DfT is still the procuring authority.*

Arriva Trains Wales operates a mix of long distance, regional and local services throughout Wales, including the Valley Lines network of lines around Cardiff, and also through services to the English border counties and to Manchester and Birmingham. The fleet consists of DMUs of Classes 142, 143, 150, 158 and 175 and two loco-hauled rakes: one used on a premium Welsh Government sponsored service on the Cardiff–Holyhead route, and one used between Manchester/Crewe and Holyhead (both are hauled by a Class 67).

| **West Midlands** | Govia (Go-Ahead/Keolis) (until 31 March 2016) | **London Midland** |
|---|---|---|

*Franchise extension to be negotiated to October 2017.*

London Midland operates long distance and regional services from London Euston to Northampton and Birmingham/Crewe and also between Birmingham and Liverpool as well as local and regional services around Birmingham, including to Stratford-upon-Avon, Worcester, Hereford, Redditch and Shrewsbury. It also operates the Bedford–Bletchley and Watford Jn–St Albans Abbey branches. The fleet consists of DMU Classes 150, 153, 170 and 172 and EMU Classes 319, 323 and 350.

The following operators run non-franchised services (* special summer services only):

| Operator | Trading Name | Route |
|---|---|---|
| BAA | Heathrow Express | London Paddington–Heathrow Airport |
| First Hull Trains | First Hull Trains | London King's Cross–Hull |
| Grand Central | Grand Central | London King's Cross–Sunderland/Bradford Interchange |
| North Yorkshire Moors Railway Enterprises | North Yorkshire Moors Railway | Pickering–Grosmont–Whitby/Battersby |
| West Coast Railway Company | West Coast Railway Company | Birmingham–Stratford-upon-Avon*<br>Fort William–Mallaig*<br>York–Settle–Carlisle* |

# INTERNATIONAL PASSENGER OPERATORS

Eurostar International operates passenger services between the UK and mainland Europe. The company, established in 2010, is jointly owned by SNCF (the national operator of France): 55%, SNCB (the national operator of Belgium): 5% and Patina Rail: 40%. Patina Rail is made up of Canadian-based Caisse de dépôt et placement du Québec (CDPG) and UK-based Hermes Infrastructure (each owning 30% and 10% respectively). This 40% was previously owned by the UK Government until it was sold in 2015.

In addition, a service for the conveyance of accompanied road vehicles through the Channel Tunnel is provided by the tunnel operating company, Eurotunnel.

# FREIGHT TRAIN OPERATORS

The following operators operate freight services or empty passenger stock workings under "Open Access" arrangements:

**Colas Rail:** Colas Rail operates a number of On-Track machines and also supplies infrastructure trains for Network Rail. It also now operates a number of different freight flows, including steel, coal, oil and timber. Colas Rail has a small but varied fleet consisting of Class 37s, 47s, 56s, 60s, 66s and 70s.

**DB Schenker Rail (UK):** Still the biggest freight operator in the country, DBS (formerly EWS before being bought by DB) provides a large number of infrastructure trains to Network Rail and also operates coal, steel, intermodal and aggregate trains nationwide. The core fleet is Class 66s. Of the original 250 ordered 176 are still used in the UK, with the remainder having moved to DB's French and Polish operations, although some of the French locos do return to the UK when major maintenance is required. A fleet of around 20–25 Class 60s are also used on heavier trains.

    DBS's six Class 59/2s are used alongside the Mendip Rail 59/0s and 59/1s on stone traffic from the Mendip quarries and around the South-East. DBS's fleet of Class 67s are used on passenger or standby duties for Arriva Trains Wales and Virgin Trains East Coast and also on excursions or special trains.

Class 90s see some use on WCML freight traffic, and are also still hired to work some Caledonian Sleeper trains. The Class 92s are used on a limited number of overnight freights on High Speed 1.

DBS also operates the Class 325 EMUs for Royal Mail and a number of excursion trains.

**Devon & Cornwall Railways** (a subsidiary of British American Railway Services): DCRail specialises in short-term freight haulage contracts, mainly in the scrap, coal and aggregates markets, using its fleet of Class 56s. It also provides locomotives from its fleet of Class 31s or 56s for stock moves or to move On-Track Machines or other equipment.

**Direct Rail Services:** DRS has built on its original nuclear flask traffic to operate a number of different services. The main flows are intermodal plus the provision of crews and locos to Network Rail for autumn Railhead Treatment Trains and also operates some NR infrastructure trains. Its Class 47s, 57s and 68s are used on excursion work.

DRS has the most varied fleet of locomotives, with Class 20s, 37s, 47s, 57s and 66s working alongside a fleet of Class 68s that are currently being delivered. The company has 32 Class 68s on order as well as ten new Vossloh electric locomotives (Class 88s), that will feature a small diesel engine.

**Freightliner:** Freightliner has two divisions: Intermodal operates container trains from the main Ports at Southampton, Felixstowe, Tilbury and Thamesport to major cities including London, Manchester, Leeds and Birmingham. The Heavy Haul division covers the movement of coal, cement, infrastructure and aggregates nationwide. Most services are worked by Class 66s, with Class 70s mainly used on some of the heavier intermodal trains. A small fleet of Class 86 and 90 electrics is used on intermodal trains on the Great Eastern and West Coast Main Lines, the Class 86s mainly being used in pairs on the WCML between Crewe and Coatbridge. Class 90s are also hired to Caledonian Sleeper.

**GB Railfreight:** GBRf, owned by Eurotunnel, operates a mixture of traffic types, mainly using Class 66s together with a small fleet of Class 73s on infrastructure duties and test trains in the South-East. A growing fleet of Class 92s is also used on some intermodal flows to/from Dollands Moor or through the Channel Tunnel to Calais. Traffic includes coal, intermodal, biomass, aggregates and gypsum as well as infrastructure services for Network Rail and London Underground. GBRf also supplies locomotives to Caledonian Sleeper.

GBRf also operates some excursion trains, including those using the preserved Class 201 "Hastings" DEMU.

**Rail Operations Group:** This new company facilitates rolling stock movements by providing drivers or using locomotives hired from other companies.

**West Coast Railway Company:** WCRC has a freight licence but doesn't operate any freight as such – only empty stock movements. Its fleet of 47s, supplemented by a smaller number of 37s and 57s, is used on excursion work nationwide, including the prestigious Royal Scotsman.

In addition Amey, Balfour Beatty Rail, Harsco Rail, South West Trains, Swietelsky Babcock Rail (SB Rail) and VolkerRail operate trains formed of On-Track Machines.

# INTRODUCTION

This book contains details of all locomotives which can run on Britain's national railway network, plus those of Eurotunnel.

Locomotives currently approved for use on the national railway network fall into the four broad types: passenger, freight, mixed traffic and shunting.

**Passenger**
The number of dedicated passenger locomotives has not changed significantly in recent years. However, the number is expected to decline in the future as new multiple unit stock replaces some of the remaining loco-hauled or propelled trains. Classes 43 (HST) and 91 and some members of Classes 57, 67, 68, 90 and 92 are dedicated to Franchised and Open Access Passenger operations. Excursion trains have a few dedicated locomotives but mainly use locomotives that are best described as mixed traffic.

**Freight**
By far the most numerous locomotives are those used solely for bulk commodity and intermodal freight. Since 1998 a large number of new Class 66 locomotives have replaced many former BR designs and in more recent years smaller numbers of Class 70s have also been introduced. There are however a significant number of BR era Class 20, 37, 47, 56, 60, 73/1, 86, 90 and 92 locomotives still in use; their number has increased slightly recently as some locomotives have been reinstated to cope with demand. In addition there is a small fleet of Class 59s acquired privately in the 1980s and 1990s and a small number of re-engined Class 57s in use.

**Mixed Traffic**
In addition to their use on passenger and commodity freight workings these locomotives are used for stock movements and specialist infrastructure and test trains. The majority, but not all, are fitted with Electric Train Supply. Locomotives from Classes 20, 31, 33, 37, 47, 57, 67, 68, 73/9 and 90 fall into this category. Also included under this heading are preserved locomotives permitted to operate on the national railway network. Although these have in the past solely operated excursion trains they are increasingly seeing occasional use on other types of trains.

**Shunting**
Very few shunting locomotives are now permitted to operate freely on the National Railway network. The small number that are have to be fitted with a plethora of safety equipment in order to have engineering acceptance. They are mainly used for local workings such as trips between yards or stock movements between depots and stations. In the main section of this book all such shunting locomotives (Classes 08 and 09) in the fleets that have permitted locomotives are included. Otherwise, shunting locomotives are not permitted to venture from depots or yards onto the national railway network other than into defined limits within interface infrastructure. Generally such locomotives, which includes an increasing number of remotely controlled driverless types, are not included in this book. However, those of BR pedigree, such as Class 08s, can be found in Section 4 – Former BR Locomotives in Industrial Service.

Locomotives which are owned by, for example, DB Schenker or Freightliner, which have been withdrawn from service and are awaiting disposal are listed in the main part of the book. Locomotives which are awaiting disposal at scrapyards are listed in the "Locomotives Awaiting Disposal" section.

Only preserved locomotives which are currently used on the National Rail network are included. Others, which may still be Network Rail registered but not at present certified for use, are not included, but will be found in the Platform 5 book, "Preserved Locomotives of British Railways".

# LAYOUT OF INFORMATION

Locomotive classes are listed in numerical order of class. Principal details and dimensions are quoted for each class in metric and/or imperial units as considered appropriate bearing in mind common UK usage.

Where numbers actually carried are different from those officially allocated, these are noted in class headings where appropriate. Where locomotives have been recently renumbered, the most immediate previous number is shown in parentheses. Each locomotive entry is laid out as in the following example:

| RSL No. | Detail | Livery | Owner | Pool | Allocn. | Name |
|---------|--------|--------|-------|------|---------|------|
| 59206 | *b | **DB** | DB | WDAM | MD | John F. Yeoman Rail Pioneer |

**Detail Differences.** Only detail differences which currently affect the areas and types of train which locomotives may work are shown. All other detail differences are excluded. Where such differences occur within a class or part class, they are shown in the "Detail" column alongside the individual locomotive number.

**Codes:** Codes are used to denote the livery, owner, pool and depot of each locomotive. Details of these will be found in section 7 of this book.

Depot allocation codes for all locomotives are shown in this book (apart from shunting locomotives (Class 08 & 09) where the actual location of each is shown). It should be noted that today much locomotive maintenance is undertaken away from these depots. This may be undertaken at fuelling points, berthing sidings or similar, or by mobile maintenance teams. Therefore locomotives in particular may not return to their "home" depots as often as in the past.

(S) denotes that the locomotive is stored (the actual location is shown).

**Names:** Only names carried with official sanction are listed. Names are shown in UPPER/lower case characters as actually shown on the name carried on the locomotive.

# GENERAL INFORMATION

## CLASSIFICATION AND NUMBERING

All locomotives are classified and allocated numbers by the Rolling Stock Library under the TOPS numbering system, introduced in 1972. This comprises a two-digit class number followed by a three-digit serial number. Where the actual number carried by a locomotive differs from the allocated number, or where an additional number is carried to the allocated number, this is shown by a note in the class heading.

For diesel locomotives, class numbers offer an indication of engine horsepower as shown in the table below.

| Class No. Range | Engine hp |
|---|---|
| 01–14 | 0–799 |
| 15–20 | 800–1000 |
| 21–31 | 1001–1499 |
| 32–39 | 1500–1999 |
| 40–54, 57 | 2000–2999 |
| 55–56, 58–70 | 3000+ |

For electric locomotives class numbers are allocated in ascending numerical order under the following scheme:

Class 71–80      Direct current and DC/diesel dual system locomotives.
Class 81 onwards    Alternating current and AC/DC dual system locomotives.

Numbers in the 89xxx series are allocated by the Rolling Stock Library to locomotives which have been deregistered but subsequently re-registered for use on the national railway network and whose original number has already been reused. 89xxx numbers are normally only carried inside locomotive cabs and are not carried externally in normal circumstances.

## WHEEL ARRANGEMENT

For main line locomotives the number of driven axles on a bogie or frame is denoted by a letter (A = 1, B = 2, C = 3 etc) and the number of non-powered axles is denoted by a number. The use of the letter "o" after a letter indicates each axle is individually powered, whilst the "+" symbol indicates bogies are inter-coupled.

For shunting locomotives, the Whyte notation is used. In this notation the number of leading wheels are given, followed by the number of driving wheels and then the trailing wheels.

## UNITS OF MEASUREMENT

All dimensions and weights are quoted for locomotives in an "as new" condition with all necessary supplies (eg oil, water and sand) on board. Dimensions are quoted in the order length x width. Lengths quoted are over buffers or couplers as appropriate. All widths quoted are maxima. Where two different wheel diameter dimensions are shown, the first refers to powered wheels and the second refers to non-powered wheels. All weights are shown as metric tonnes (t = tonnes).

# HAULAGE CAPABILITY OF DIESEL LOCOMOTIVES

The haulage capability of a diesel locomotive depends upon three basic factors:

1. Adhesive weight. The greater the weight on the driving wheels, the greater the adhesion and more tractive power can be applied before wheelslip occurs.

2. The characteristics of its transmission. To start a train the locomotive has to exert a pull at standstill. A direct drive diesel engine cannot do this, hence the need for transmission. This may be mechanical, hydraulic or electric. The present British Standard for locomotives is electric transmission. Here the diesel engine drives a generator or alternator and the current produced is fed to the traction motors. The force produced by each driven wheel depends on the current in its traction motor. In other words, the larger the current, the harder it pulls. As the locomotive speed increases, the current in the traction motor falls, hence the *Maximum Tractive Effort* is the maximum force at its wheels the locomotive can exert at a standstill. The electrical equipment cannot take such high currents for long without overheating. Hence the *Continuous Tractive Effort* is quoted which represents the current which the equipment can take continuously.

3. The power of its engine. Not all power reaches the rail, as electrical machines are approximately 90% efficient. As the electrical energy passes through two such machines (the generator or alternator and the traction motors), the *Power at Rail* is approximately 81% (90% of 90%) of the engine power, less a further amount used for auxiliary equipment such as radiator fans, traction motor blowers, air compressors, battery charging, cab heating, Electric Train Supply (ETS) etc. The power of the locomotive is proportional to the tractive effort times the speed. Hence when on full power there is a speed corresponding to the continuous tractive effort.

# HAULAGE CAPABILITY OF ELECTRIC LOCOMOTIVES

Unlike a diesel locomotive, an electric locomotive does not develop its power on board and its performance is determined only by two factors, namely its weight and the characteristics of its electrical equipment. Whereas a diesel locomotive tends to be a constant power machine, the power of an electric locomotive varies considerably. Up to a certain speed it can produce virtually a constant tractive effort. Hence power rises with speed according to the formula given in section three above, until a maximum speed is reached at which tractive effort falls, such that the power also falls. Hence the power at the speed corresponding to the maximum tractive effort is lower than the maximum speed.

# BRAKE FORCE

The brake force is a measure of the braking power of a locomotive. This is shown on the locomotive data panels so operating staff can ensure sufficient brake power is available on freight trains.

# ELECTRIC TRAIN SUPPLY (ETS)

A number of locomotives are equipped to provide a supply of electricity to the train being hauled to power auxiliaries such as heating, cooling fans, air conditioning and kitchen equipment. ETS is provided from the locomotive by means of a separate alternator (except Class 33 locomotives, which have a DC generator). The ETS index of a locomotive is a measure of the electrical power available for train supply. Class 55 locomotives provide an ETS directly from one of their traction generators into the train line.

Similarly, most loco-hauled carriages also have an ETS index, which in this case is a measure of the power required to operate equipment mounted in the carriage. The sum of the ETS indices of all the hauled vehicles in a train must not exceed the ETS index of the locomotive.

ETS is commonly (but incorrectly) known as ETH (Electric Train Heating), which is a throwback to the days before loco-hauled carriages were equipped with electrically powered auxiliary equipment other than for train heating.

# ROUTE AVAILABILITY (RA)

This is a measure of a railway vehicle's axle load. The higher the axle load of a vehicle, the higher the RA number on a scale from 1 to 10. Each Network Rail route has a RA number and in general no vehicle with a higher RA number may travel on that route without special clearance.

# MULTIPLE WORKING

Multiple working between vehicles (ie two or more powered vehicles being driven from one cab) is facilitated by jumper cables connecting the vehicles. However, not all types of locomotive are compatible with each other, and a number of different systems are in use. Some are compatible with others, some are not. BR used "multiple working codes" to designate which locomotives were compatible. The list below shows which classes of locomotives are compatible with each other – the former BR multiple working code being shown in brackets. It should be noted that some locomotives have had the equipment removed or made inoperable.

**With other classes:**
Classes 20, 25, 31, 33, 37 40 & 73/1*. (Blue Star)
Classes 56 & 58. (Red Diamond)
Classes 59, 66, 67, 68, 70 & 73/9.
* DRS has since adapted the systems so its Classes 20/3, 37, 47 & 57 can work with each other only.

**With other members of same class only:**
Class 43, Class 47 (Green Circle), Class 50 (Orange Square), Class 60.

# PUSH-PULL OPERATION

Some locomotives are modified to operate passenger and service (formed of laboratory, test and inspection carriages) trains in "push-pull" mode – which allows the train to be driven from either end – either with locomotives at each end (both under power) or with a driving brake van at one end and a locomotive at the other. Various different systems are now in use. Electric locomotive Classes 86, 87, 90 & 91 use a time-division multiplex (TDM) system for push-pull working which utilises the existing RCH jumper cables fitted to carriages. Previously these cables had only been used to control train lighting and public address systems. Class 47 locomotives 47701– 47717 were equipped with an older non-standard TDM system.

More recently locomotive of Classes 67 and 68 have used the Association of American Railroads (AAR) system.

# ABBREVIATIONS

Standard abbreviations used in this book are:

| | |
|---|---|
| a | Train air brake equipment only. |
| b | Drophead buckeye couplers. |
| c | Scharfenberg couplers. |
| d | Fitted with retractable Dellner couplers. |
| e | European Railway Traffic Management System (ERTMS) signalling equipment fitted. |
| k | Fitted with Swinghead Automatic "buckeye" combination couplers. |
| p | Train air, vacuum and electro-pneumatic brakes. |
| r | Radio Electric Token Block signalling equipment fitted. |
| s | Slow Speed Control equipment. |
| t | tonnes |
| v | Train vacuum brake only. |
| x | Train air and vacuum brakes ("Dual brakes"). |
| + | Additional fuel tank capacity. |
| § | Sandite laying equipment. |

In all cases use of the above abbreviations indicates the equipment in question is normally operable. The definition of non-standard abbreviations and symbols is detailed in individual class headings.

# 1. DIESEL LOCOMOTIVES

## CLASS 08          BR/ENGLISH ELECTRIC          0-6-0

**Built:** 1955–62 by BR at Crewe, Darlington, Derby Locomotive, Doncaster or Horwich Works.
**Engine:** English Electric 6KT of 298 kW (400 hp) at 680 rpm.
**Main Generator:** English Electric 801.
**Traction Motors:** Two English Electric 506.
**Maximum Tractive Effort:** 156 kN (35000 lbf).
**Continuous Tractive Effort:** 49 kN (11100 lbf) at 8.8 mph.
**Power at Rail:** 194 kW (260 hp).          **Train Brakes:** Air & vacuum.
**Brake Force:** 19 t.                       **Dimensions:** 8.92 x 2.59 m.
**Weight:** 49.6–50.4 t.                     **Wheel Diameter:** 1372 mm.
**Design Speed:** 20 mph.                    **Maximum Speed:** 15 mph.
**Fuel Capacity:** 3037 litres.              **RA:** 5.
**Train Supply:** Not equipped.

† – Fitted with remote control equipment.

For shunting locomotives, instead of the two-letter depot code, actual locations at the time of publication are given.

Class 08s that don't have current Network Rail engineering acceptance and are considered to be "in industrial service" can be found in section 4 of this book.

08850 has acceptance for use between Battersby and Whitby only, for rescue purposes.

**Non-standard liveries/numbering:**

08480   Yellow with a red bodyside band. Carries number "TOTON No 1".
08616   Carries number 3783.
08696   Carries no number.
08701   Carries number "Tyne 100".
08721   As **B**, but with a black roof & "EXPRESS PARCELS" branding with red & yellow stripe.
08824   Carries number "IEMD01".
08899   Crimson lake.

Originally numbered in series D3000–D4192.

**Class 08/0. Standard Design.**

| 08405 | a † | **E**  | DB | WQAA | Crewe International Depot (S)    |
|-------|-----|--------|----|------|---------------------------------|
| 08410 | a   | **GW** | FW | EFSH | Plymouth Laira Depot            |
| 08417 | a   | **Y**  | NR | QADD | RVEL Derby                      |
| 08428 | ak  | **E**  | DB | WSSC | Warrington Yards (S)            |
| 08451 |     | **B**  | AM | ATLO | Manchester Longsight Depot      |
| 08454 |     | **K**  | AM | ATLO | Liverpool Edge Hill Depot       |
| 08472 | a   | **WA** | WA | RFSH | Edinburgh Craigentinny Depot    |
| 08480 | a   | **0**  | DB | WQAA | Toton Depot (S)                 |
| 08483 | a   | **K**  | FW | EFSH | Old Oak Common HST Depot        |

▲ Departmental grey-liveried 08645 at Laira depot on 20/09/14. **Robert Pritchard**

▼ The two Class 08 shunters based at Polmadie depot, 08954 in BR Blue livery and 08696 in green livery are seen on 05/11/14. **Robin Ralston**

▲ Revised DRS-liveried 20308 and 20312 top-and-tail the 3S14 11.17 Grimsby Town–Malton RHTT train near Wombwell on 10/10/14. **Aubrey Evans**

▼ Devon & Cornwall Railways Silver-liveried 31601 arrives at Brush Loughborough hauling Chiltern Railways DVT 82304 from Wembley on 16/06/15. **Jamie Squibbs**

▲ Superbly restored into BR Revised blue livery, 37401 heads south from St Bees with the 11.56 Carlisle–Lancaster Northern service on 01/08/15.

**Robert Pritchard**

▲ West Coast Railway Company Maroon-liveried 37706 at Weymouth with a Cathedrals Express excursion on 09/07/15. **Stephen Ginn**

▼ Virgin Trains East Coast-liveried 43310 (with 43311 on the rear) arrives at York with the 07.30 Edinburgh–London King's Cross on 22/09/15. **Robert Pritchard**

▲ In the new Great Western Railway green livery, HST power cars 43187 and 43188 approach Whiteball Tunnel with the 10.00 Penzance–Paddington on 29/09/15.

**Tony Christie**

▲ West Coast Railway Company Maroon-liveried 47851 passes Sandiacre with a Norwich–Liverpool Lime Street Nenta railtour on 18/07/15.　　**Steve Donald**

▼ Railfreight grey 56104, owned by UK Rail Leasing, passes Oakley with 6Y56 10.35 Butterley–Toton "Railvac" movement on 09/07/15.　　**Nigel Gibbs**

▲ BR Blue-liveried 55022 (running as long-scrapped 55003 "Meld") passes Achnabone Farm with the Spean Bridge–Mallaig leg of the Royal Scotsman luxury train on 02/05/15. **Andrew Mason**

▲ New DRS-liveried 57301 passes Norton, near Worcester, with a 15.53 Oxford–Hooton railtour on 11/04/15. **Steve Widdowson**

▼ DB Schenker-liveried 59205 and Hanson Quarry Products-liveried 59103 double head the 13.30 Appleford–Whatley stone empties on the approach to Frome on 25/06/15. **Glen Batten**

| 08495 † | E | DB | WQBA | Crewe International Depot (S) |
|---|---|---|---|---|
| 08523 | RS | RL | MRSO | Inverness Depot |
| 08525 | ST | EM | EMSL | Leeds Neville Hill Depot |
| 08530 | FL | P | DFLS | Felixstowe FLT |
| 08531 a | FH | P | DFLS | Felixstowe FLT |
| 08567 † | E | DB | WQDA | Crewe International Depot (S) |
| 08571 a | WA | WA | HBSH | Bounds Green Depot |
| 08575 | FL | P | DHLT | LH Group, Barton-under-Needwood (S) |
| 08578 † | E | DB | WQDA | Toton Depot (S) |
| 08580 | E | DB | WQDA | Bescot Yards (S) |
| 08585 | FL | P | DFLS | LH Group, Barton-under-Needwood |
| 08593 | E | DB | WQDA | Crewe International Depot (S) |
| 08596 a† | WA | WA | HBSH | Bounds Green Depot |
| 08605 † | E | DB | WQBA | Toton Depot (S) |
| 08611 | V | AM | ATLO | Manchester Longsight Depot |
| 08615 | WA | WA | RFSH | Edinburgh Craigentinny Depot |
| 08616 | LM | LM | EJLO | Birmingham Tyseley Depot |
| 08617 | K | AM | ATLO | Wembley Depot |
| 08623 | DB | DB | WSSC | Hoo Junction Yards |
| 08624 | FL | P | DFLS | Trafford Park FLT |
| 08630 | E | DB | WQCA | Toton Yards (S) |
| 08632 † | DB | DB | WSRC | Mossend Yards |
| 08633 † | E | DB | WQCA | Axiom Rail, Stoke-on-Trent Works |
| 08641 | B | FW | EFSH | Penzance Long Rock Depot |
| 08644 | B | FW | EFSH | RVEL Derby |
| 08645 | DG | FW | EFSH | Plymouth Laira Depot |
| 08653 | E | DB | WQDA | Toton Yards (S) |
| 08663 a | B | FW | EFSH | Bristol St Philip's Marsh Depot |
| 08669 a | WA | WA | RFSH | Wabtec Rail, Doncaster Works |
| 08676 † | E | DB | WQBA | Toton Depot (S) |
| 08690 | ST | EM | EMSL | Leeds Neville Hill Depot |
| 08691 | FL | FL | DFLS | Southampton Maritime FLT |
| 08696 a | G | AM | ATLO | Glasgow Polmadie Depot |
| 08701 a† | RX | DB | WQDA | Toton Yards (S) |
| 08703 a | E | DB | WSSC | Knottingley Depot |
| 08706 † | E | DB | WQCA | Crewe International Depot (S) |
| 08709 | E | DB | WQDA | Bescot Yards (S) |
| 08714 | E | DB | WQDA | Crewe International Depot (S) |
| 08721 | O | AM | ATLO | Eastleigh Works |
| 08724 | WA | WA | HBSH | Wabtec Rail, Doncaster Works |
| 08735 † | E | DB | WQCA | Eastleigh Yards (S) |
| 08737 a† | E | DB | WQBA | Crewe International Depot (S) |
| 08742 † | RX | DB | WSSC | Oxford Hinksey Yard |
| 08752 † | E | DB | WSSC | Tyne Yard |
| 08754 | B | RL | MRSO | Norwich Crown Point Depot |
| 08757 † | RG | DB | WQBA | Crewe International Depot (S) |
| 08782 a† | CU | DB | WQBA | Doncaster Yards (S) |
| 08784 † | E | DB | WQBA | Toton Depot (S) |
| 08785 a | FL | P | DFLS | Southampton Maritime FLT |
| 08788 | K | RL | MRSO | Inverness Depot |
| 08790 | B | AM | ATLO | Wolverhampton Oxley Depot |

| 08795 | **K** | FW | EFSH | Swansea Landore Depot |
| 08799 a | **E** | DB | WSSC | Westbury Yards |
| 08802 † | **E** | DB | WQAA | Toton Depot (S) |
| 08804 † | **E** | DB | WQBA | Crewe International Depot (S) |
| 08805 | **FO** | LM | EJLO | Birmingham Soho Depot |
| 08822 | **IC** | FW | EFSH | Bristol St Philip's Marsh Depot |
| 08824 ak | **K** | DB | WQDA | Crewe International Depot (S) |
| 08836 | **GW** | FW | EFSH | Old Oak Common HST Depot |
| 08847 | **CD** | RL | MRSO | Norwich Crown Point Depot |
| 08850 | **B** | NY | MBDL | Grosmont Depot |
| 08853 a | **WA** | WA | RFSH | Wabtec Rail, Doncaster Works |
| 08865 | **E** | DB | WQDA | Crewe International Depot (S) |
| 08874 | **SL** | RL | MRSO | Tata Steel, Shotton Works |
| 08879 † | **E** | DB | WSRC | Margam Yards |
| 08886 | **E** | DB | WQCA | Crewe International Depot (S) |
| 08887 a | **B** | AM | ATLO | Wembley Depot |
| 08888 † | **E** | DB | WQAA | Bescot Yards (S) |
| 08891 | **FL** | P | DHLT | LH Group, Barton-under-Needwood (S) |
| 08899 | **0** | EM | EMSL | Derby Etches Park Depot |
| 08904 | **E** | DB | WSGC | Eastleigh Yards |
| 08907 | **DB** | DB | WQBA | Bescot Yards (S) |
| 08908 | **ST** | EM | EMSL | Leeds Neville Hill Depot |
| 08922 | **DG** | DB | WQBA | Toton Depot (S) |
| 08925 | **G** | GB | GBWM | Cardiff Tidal Steelworks |
| 08934 a | **VP** | GB | GBWM | March Whitemoor Yard |
| 08948 c | **EP** | EU | GPSS | Temple Mills Depot |
| 08950 | **ST** | EM | EMSL | Leeds Neville Hill Depot |
| 08954 | **B** | AM | ATLO | Glasgow Polmadie Depot |

---

# CLASS 09          BR/ENGLISH ELECTRIC          0-6-0

**Built:** 1959–62 by BR at Darlington or Horwich Works.
**Engine:** English Electric 6KT of 298 kW (400 hp) at 680 rpm.
**Main Generator:** English Electric 801.
**Traction Motors:** English Electric 506.
**Maximum Tractive Effort:** 111 kN (25000 lbf).
**Continuous Tractive Effort:** 39 kN (8800 lbf) at 11.6 mph.
**Power at Rail:** 201 kW (269 hp).          **Train Brakes:** Air & vacuum.
**Brake Force:** 19 t.                              **Dimensions:** 8.92 x 2.59 m.
**Weight:** 49 t.                                       **Wheel Diameter:** 1372 mm.
**Design Speed:** 27 mph.                        **Maximum Speed:** 27 mph.
**Fuel Capacity:** 3037 litres.                  **RA:** 5.
**Train Supply:** Not equipped.

Class 09s that don't have current Network Rail engineering acceptance and are considered to be "in industrial service" can be found in section 4 of this book.

Class 09/0 were originally numbered D3665–D3671, D3719–D3721, D4099–D4114.

**Class 09/0. Built as Class 09.**

| | | | | |
|---|---|---|---|---|
| 09002 | **G** | GB | GBWM | March Whitemoor Yard |
| 09009 | **G** | GB | GBWM | Eastleigh Works |
| 09026 a | **G** | GV | MBDL | Brighton Lovers Walk Depot |

**Class 09/1. Converted from Class 08. 110 V electrical equipment.**
**Converted:** 1992–1993 by RFS Industries, Kilnhurst.

| | | | | |
|---|---|---|---|---|
| 09106 (08759) | **DB** | DB | WSSC | Knottingley Depot |

**Class 08 and Class 09 names:**

| | |
|---|---|
| 08451 | M.A. SMITH |
| 08483 | NEIL / SCOUSEY |
| | Neil Morgan 1964–2014 |
| | Team Leader O.O.C. |
| 08495 | NOEL KIRTON OBE |
| 08525 | DUNCAN BEDFORD |
| 08585 | Vicky |
| 08611 | LONGSIGHT TMD |
| 08616 | TYSELEY 100 |
| 08630 | BOB BROWN |
| 08644 | Laira Diesel Depot |
| | 50 Years 1962–2012 |
| 08645 | Mike Baggott |
| 08669 | Bob Machin |
| 08690 | DAVID THIRKILL |
| 08691 | Terri |
| 08721 | DOWNHILL C.S. |
| 08782 | CASTLETON WORKS |
| 08790 | Steve Purser |
| 08799 | FRED |
| 08822 | John |
| 08874 | Catherine |
| 08899 | Midland Counties Railway |
| | 175 1839–2014 |
| 08908 | IVAN STEPHENSON |
| 08950 | DAVID LIGHTFOOT |
| 09026 | Cedric Wares |

## CLASS 20     ENGLISH ELECTRIC     Bo-Bo

**Built:** 1957–68 by English Electric at Vulcan Foundry, Newton-le-Willows or by Robert Stephenson & Hawthorns at Darlington.
**Engine:** English Electric 8SVT Mk II of 746 kW (1000 hp) at 850 rpm.
**Main Generator:** English Electric 819/3C.
**Traction Motors:** English Electric 526/5D or 526/8D.
**Maximum Tractive Effort:** 187 kN (42000 lbf).
**Continuous Tractive Effort:** 111 kN (25000 lbf) at 11 mph.

| | |
|---|---|
| **Power at Rail:** 574 kW (770 hp). | **Train Brakes:** Air & vacuum. |
| **Brake Force:** 35 t. | **Dimensions:** 14.25 x 2.67 m. |
| **Weight:** 73.4–73.5 t. | **Wheel Diameter:** 1092 mm. |
| **Design Speed:** 75 mph. | **Maximum Speed:** 75 mph. |
| **Fuel Capacity:** 1727 litres. | **RA:** 5. |
| **Train Supply:** Not equipped. | |

Class 20s that don't have current Network Rail engineering acceptance and are considered to be "in industrial service" can be found in section 4 of this book.

Originally numbered in series D8007–D8190, D8315–D8325.

**Non-standard liveries/numbering:**

20088 RFS grey (carries No. 2017).
20227 White, red & blue with London Underground roundels.

**Class 20/0. Standard Design.**

| | | | | | |
|---|---|---|---|---|---|
| 20016 | B | HN | HNRS | LM (S) | |
| 20081 | B | HN | HNRS | LM (S) | |
| 20088 | 0 | HN | HNRS | LM (S) | |
| 20092 | U | HN | HNRS | LM (S) | |
| 20096 | B | HN | GBEE | BH | |
| 20107 | B | HN | GBEE | BH | |
| 20118 | F0 | HN | GBEE | BH | Saltburn-by-the-Sea |
| 20132 | F0 | HN | GBEE | BH | Barrow Hill Depot |
| 20142 | B | 20 | GBEE | SK | |
| 20189 | B | 20 | GBEE | SK | |
| 20205 | B | 2L | MOLO | SK | |
| 20227 | 0 | 2L | MOLO | SK | |

**Class 20/3. Direct Rail Services refurbished locos.** Details as Class 20/0 except:

**Refurbished:** 15 locomotives were refurbished 1995–96 by Brush Traction at Loughborough (20301–305) or 1997–98 by RFS(E) at Doncaster (20306–315). Disc indicators or headcode panels removed.

**Train Brakes:** Air.                    **Maximum Speed:** 60 mph (+ 75 mph).
**Weight:** 73 t (+ 76 t).                **Fuel Capacity:** 2909 (+ 4909) litres.
**Brake Force:** 35 t (+ 31 t).           **RA:** 5 (+ 6).

| | | | | | |
|---|---|---|---|---|---|
| 20301 | (20047) r | DS | DR | XHSS | BH (S) | Max Joule 1958–1999 |
| 20302 | (20084) r | DS | DR | XHNC | KM | |
| 20303 | (20127) r | DS | DR | XHNC | KM | |
| 20304 | (20120) r | DS | DR | XHSS | KM (S) | |
| 20305 | (20095) r | DS | DR | XHNC | KM | Gresty Bridge |
| 20308 | (20187) r+ | DS | DR | XHNC | KM | |
| 20309 | (20075) r+ | DS | DR | XHNC | KM | |
| 20311 | (20102) r+ | HN | HN | GBEE | BH | |
| 20312 | (20042) r+ | DS | DR | XHSS | CR (S) | |
| 20314 | (20117) r+ | HN | HN | GBEE | BH | |

**Class 20/9. Harry Needle Railroad Company (former Hunslet-Barclay/ DRS) locos.** Details as Class 20/0 except:

**Refurbished:** 1989 by Hunslet-Barclay at Kilmarnock.
**Train Brakes:** Air.                    **Fuel Capacity:** 1727 (+ 4727) litres.
**RA:** 5 (+ 6).

| | | | | | |
|---|---|---|---|---|---|
| 20901 | (20101) | GB | HN | GBEE | BH | |
| 20903 | (20083) + | DR | HN | HNRS | BO (S) | |
| 20904 | (20041) | DR | HN | HNRS | BO (S) | |
| 20905 | (20225) + | GB | HN | GBEE | BH | |

# CLASS 25   BR/BEYER PEACOCK/SULZER                Bo-Bo

**Built:** 1965 by Beyer Peacock at Gorton.
**Engine:** Sulzer 6LDA28-B of 930 kW (1250 hp) at 750 rpm.
**Main Generator:** AEI RTB15656.          **Traction Motors:** AEI 253AY.
**Maximum Tractive Effort:** 200 kN (45000 lbf).
**Continuous Tractive Effort:** 93 kN (20800 lbf) at 17.1 mph.

**Power at Rail:** 708 kW (949 hp).
**Brake Force:** 38 t.
**Weight:** 71.5 t.
**Design Speed:** 90 mph.
**Fuel Capacity:** 2270 litres.
**Train Supply:** Not equipped.

**Train Brakes:** Air & vacuum.
**Dimensions:** 15.39 x 2.73 m.
**Wheel Diameter:** 1143 mm.
**Maximum Speed:** 60 mph.
**RA:** 5.

Original number is D7628, which the locomotive currently carries.

Only certified for use on Network Rail metals between Whitby and Battersby, as an extension of North Yorkshire Moors Railway services.

| 25278 | **GG** | NY | MBDL | NY | SYBILLA |

# CLASS 31   BRUSH/ENGLISH ELECTRIC   A1A-A1A

**Built:** 1958–62 by Brush Traction at Loughborough.
**Engine:** English Electric 12SVT of 1100 kW (1470 hp) at 850 rpm.
**Main Generator:** Brush TG160-48.   **Traction Motors:** Brush TM73-68.
**Maximum Tractive Effort:** 160 kN (35900 lbf).
**Continuous Tractive Effort:** 83 kN (18700 lbf) at 23.5 mph.
**Power at Rail:** 872 kW (1170 hp).
**Brake Force:** 49 t.
**Weight:** 106.7–111 t.
**Design Speed:** 90 mph.
**Fuel Capacity:** 2409 litres.
**Train Supply:** Not equipped.

**Train Brakes:** Air & vacuum.
**Dimensions:** 17.30 x 2.67 m.
**Wheel Diameter:** 1092/1003 mm.
**Maximum Speed:** 90 mph.
**RA:** 5 or 6.

Originally numbered D5520–D5699, D5800–D5862 (not in order).

**Non-standard liveries/numbering:**

31190 Also carries number D5613.
31452 DCR green.

**Class 31/1. Standard Design.** RA: 5.

| 31105 | **Y** | NR | QADD | ZA (S) | |
| 31106 a | **B** | HJ | RVLO | ZA (S) | |
| 31128 | **B** | NS | NRLO | BO | CHARYBDIS |
| 31190 | **G** | BA | HTLX | WH | |
| 31233 a | **Y** | NR | QADD | EC (S) | |
| 31285 | **Y** | NR | QADD | EX (S) | |

**Class 31/4. Electric Train Supply equipment.** RA: 6.
**Train Supply:** Electric, index 66.

| 31452 | **O** | BA | HTLX | ZA | |
| 31454 | **IC** | BA | HTLX | WH (S) | |
| 31459 | **K** | BA | RVLO | ZA (S) | CERBERUS |
| 31465 | **Y** | NR | QADD | ZA (S) | |
| 31468 | **FR** | BA | RVLO | WO (S) | HYDRA |

**Class 31/6. ETS through wiring and controls.** RA: 5.

| 31601 (31186) | **DC** | BA | HTLX | WH | Devon Diesel Society |
| 31602 (31191) | **Y** | BA | HTLX | WO (S) | |

## CLASS 33    BRCW/SULZER    Bo-Bo

**Built:** 1960–62 by the Birmingham Railway Carriage & Wagon Company at Smethwick.
**Engine:** Sulzer 8LDA28 of 1160 kW (1550 hp) at 750 rpm.
**Main Generator:** Crompton Parkinson CG391B1.
**Traction Motors:** Crompton Parkinson C171C2.
**Maximum Tractive Effort:** 200 kN (45000 lbf).
**Continuous Tractive Effort:** 116 kN (26000 lbf) at 17.5 mph.
**Power at Rail:** 906 kW (1215 hp).     **Train Brakes:** Air & vacuum.
**Brake Force:** 35 t.                   **Dimensions:** 15.47 x 2.82 (2.64 m 33/2).
**Weight:** 76-78 t.                     **Wheel Diameter:** 1092 mm.
**Design Speed:** 85 mph.                **Maximum Speed:** 85 mph.
**Fuel Capacity:** 3410 litres.          **RA:** 6.
**Train Supply:** Electric, index 48 (750 V DC only).

Originally numbered in series D6500–D6597 but not in order.

**Non-standard numbering:** 33012 Carries number D6515.

**Class 33/0. Standard Design.**

| | | | | | |
|---|---|---|---|---|---|
| 33012 | **G** | 71 | MBDL | Swanage Rly | Lt Jenny Lewis RN |
| 33025 | **WC** | WC | AWCX | SH (S) | Glen Falloch |
| 33029 | **WC** | WC | AWCX | CS (S) | |
| 33030 | **DR** | WC | AWCX | CS (S) | |

**Class 33/2. Built to former Loading Gauge of Tonbridge–Battle Line.**
Equipped with slow speed control.

| | | | | | |
|---|---|---|---|---|---|
| 33207 | **WC** | WC | AWCX | CS (S) | Jim Martin |

## CLASS 37    ENGLISH ELECTRIC    Co-Co

**Built:** 1960–66 by English Electric at Vulcan Foundry, Newton-le-Willows or by Robert Stephenson & Hawthorns at Darlington.
**Engine:** English Electric 12CSVT of 1300 kW (1750 hp) at 850 rpm.
**Main Generator:** English Electric 822/10G.
**Traction Motors:** English Electric 538/A.
**Maximum Tractive Effort:** 247 kN (55500 lbf).
**Continuous Tractive Effort:** 156 kN (35000 lbf) at 13.6 mph.
**Power at Rail:** 932 kW (1250 hp).     **Train Brakes:** Air & vacuum.
**Brake Force:** 50 t.                   **Dimensions:** 18.75 x 2.74 m.
**Weight:** 102.8–108.4 t.               **Wheel Diameter:** 1092 mm.
**Design Speed:** 90 mph.                **Maximum Speed:** 80 mph.
**Fuel Capacity:** 4046 (+ 7683) litres. **RA:** 5 (§ 6).
**Train Supply:** Not equipped.

Originally numbered D6600–D6608, D6700–D6999 (not in order).

**Non-standard numbering:**

37057  Also carries the number D6757.
37905  Also carries the number D6838.

**Class 37/0. Standard Design.** Details as above.

| | | | | | |
|---|---|---|---|---|---|
| 37038 a | **DR** | DR | XHSS | BH (S) | |
| 37057 | **G** | CS | COTS | RU | |
| 37059 ar+ | **DI** | DR | XHNC | KM | |
| 37069 ar+ | **DS** | DR | XHNC | KM | |
| 37116 + | **B** | CS | COTS | RU | |
| 37146 | **CE** | CS | COLS | Leeming Bar (S) | |
| 37165 a+ | **CE** | WC | AWCX | CS (S) | |
| 37175 a | **CS** | CS | COTS | RU | |
| 37188 | **F** | CS | COLS | Rowsley (S) | |
| 37194 a+ | **DS** | DR | XHSS | ZA (S) | |
| 37198 + | **Y** | NR | MBDL | BO (S) | CHIEF ENGINEER |
| 37207 | **CE** | CS | COLS | BH (S) | |
| 37214 | **WC** | WC | AWCX | CS (S) | |
| 37218 ar+ | **DI** | DR | XHNC | KM | |
| 37219 | **CS** | CS | COTS | RU | |
| 37254 | **IC** | CS | COLS | BH (S) | |
| 37259 ar | **DS** | DR | XHNC | KM | |

**Class 37/4. Refurbished with electric train supply equipment.** Main generator replaced by alternator. Regeared (CP7) bogies. Details as Class 37/0 except:
**Main Alternator:** Brush BA1005A.     **Power At Rail:** 935 kW (1254 hp).
**Traction Motors:** English Electric 538/5A.
**Maximum Tractive Effort:** 256 kN (57440 lbf).
**Continuous Tractive Effort:** 184 kN (41250 lbf) at 11.4 mph.
**Weight:** 107 t.            **Design Speed:** 80 mph.
**Fuel Capacity:** 7683 litres.
**Train Supply:** Electric, index 30.

| | | | | | |
|---|---|---|---|---|---|
| 37401 ar | **BL** | DR | XHAC | KM | Mary Queen of Scots |
| 37402 a | **DS** | DR | XHAC | KM | Stephen Middlemore 23.12.1954–8.6.2013 |
| 37405 ar | **DS** | DR | XHAC | KM | |
| 37407 | **F** | DR | XHSS | ZA (S) | |
| 37409 ar | **DS** | DR | XHAC | KM | Lord Hinton |
| 37413 | **E** | DR | XHSS | ZA (S) | |
| 37419 ar | **DS** | DR | XHAC | KM | Carl Haviland 1954–2012 |
| 37421 | **CS** | CS | COTS | RU | |
| 37422 ar | **DR** | DR | XHAC | KM | |
| 37423 ar | **DI** | DR | XHAC | KM | Spirit of the Lakes |
| 37424 | **F** | DR | XHSS | ZA (S) | |
| 37425 ar | **DS** | DR | XHAC | KM | Sir Robert McAlpine/Concrete Bob |

**Class 37/5. Refurbished without train supply equipment.** Main generator replaced by alternator. Regeared (CP7) bogies. Details as Class 37/4 except:
**Power At Rail:** 932 kW (1250 hp).
**Maximum Tractive Effort:** 248 kN (55590 lbf).
**Continuous Tractive Effort:** 184 kN (41250 lbf) at 11.4 mph.
**Weight:** 106.1–110.0 t.

| | | | | | |
|---|---|---|---|---|---|
| 37503 r§ | **E** | DR | XHHP | BH (S) | |
| 37510 a | **DS** | DR | XHSS | BH (S) | |
| 37516 s | **WC** | WC | AWCA | CS | Loch Laidon |

| 37517 | as | **LH** | WC | AWCX | CS (S) | |
|--------|------|--------|------|--------|---------|---|
| 37518 | ar | **WC** | WC | AWCA | CS | |
| 37521 | r§ | **E** | DR | XHHP | BH (S) | English China Clays |

**Class 37/6. Originally refurbished for Nightstar services.** Main generator replaced by alternator. UIC jumpers. Details as Class 37/5 except:

**Maximum Speed:** 90 mph.        **Train Brake:** Air.
**Train Supply:** Not equipped, but electric through wired.

| 37601 | a | **DS** | DR | XHNC | KM | Class 37-'Fifty' |
|--------|------|--------|------|--------|------|---|
| 37602 | ar | **DS** | DR | XHNC | KM | |
| 37603 | a | **DS** | DR | XHNC | KM | |
| 37604 | a | **DS** | DR | XHNC | KM | |
| 37605 | ar | **DS** | DR | XHNC | KM | |
| 37606 | a | **DS** | DR | XHNC | KM | |
| 37607 | ar | **DS** | DR | XHNC | KM | |
| 37608 | ar | **DS** | DR | XHNC | KM | |
| 37609 | a | **DI** | DR | XHNC | KM | |
| 37610 | ar | **DS** | DR | XHNC | KM | T.S.(Ted) Cassady 14.5.61–6.4.08 |
| 37611 | a | **DS** | DR | XHNC | KM | |
| 37612 | a | **DS** | DR | XHNC | KM | |

**Class 37/5 continued.**

| 37667 | arst | **DS** | DR | XHNC | KM | |
|--------|------|--------|------|--------|---------|---|
| 37668 | e | **WC** | WC | AWCA | CS | |
| 37669 | e | **WC** | WC | AWCA | CS | |
| 37670 | r | **DB** | DR | XHSS | BH (S) | |
| 37676 | a | **WC** | WC | AWCA | CS (S) | Loch Rannoch |
| 37682 | ar | **DS** | DR | XHSS | ZA (S) | |
| 37685 | a | **WC** | WC | AWCA | CS | Loch Arkaig |
| 37688 | art | **DS** | DR | XHNC | KM | Kingmoor TMD |

**Class 37/7. Refurbished locos. Main generator replaced by alternator. Regeared (CP7) bogies.** Ballast weights added. Details as Class 37/5 except:
**Main Alternator:** GEC G564AZ (37796–803) Brush BA1005A (others).
**Maximum Tractive Effort:** 276 kN (62000 lbf).
**Weight:** 120 t.        **RA:** 7.

| 37703 | | **DR** | DR | XHHP | Bo'ness | |
|--------|------|--------|------|--------|---------|---|
| 37706 | | **WC** | WC | AWCA | CS | |
| 37710 | | **LH** | WC | AWCX | CS (S) | |
| 37712 | a | **WC** | WC | AWCX | CS (S) | |
| 37714 | | **DR** | DR | XHHP | Daventry | |
| 37716 | | **DI** | DR | XHHP | ZA (S) | |
| 37800 | | **GIF** | EP | EPUK | LR (S) | |
| 37884 | | **EX** | EP | EPUK | LR | |

**Class 97/3. Class 37s refurbished for Network Rail for use on the Cambrian Lines which are signalled by ERTMS.** Details as Class 37/0.

| 97301 | (37100) | e | **Y** | NR | QETS | ZA | |
|--------|---------|------|------|------|--------|------|---|
| 97302 | (37170) | e | **Y** | NR | QETS | ZA | |
| 97303 | (37178) | e | **Y** | NR | QETS | ZA | |
| 97304 | (37217) | e | **Y** | NR | QETS | ZA | John Tiley |

**Class 37/9. Refurbished locos. New power unit. Main generator replaced by alternator.** Ballast weights added. Details as Class 37/4 except:
**Engine:** Ruston RK270T of 1340 kW (1800 hp) at 900 rpm.
**Main Alternator:** Brush BA15005A.
**Train supply:** Not equipped.
**Maximum Tractive Effort:** 279 kN (62680 lbf).
Continuous Tractive Effort: 184 kN (41250 lbf) at 11.4 mph.
**Weight:** 120 t.                              **RA:** 7.

| 37905 | **G**  | UK | UKRO | LR (S) |
| 37906 | **FO** | UK | UKRS | LR (S) |

# CLASS 40         ENGLISH ELECTRIC         1Co-Co1

**Built:** 1958–62 by English Electric at Vulcan Foundry, Newton-le-Willows.
**Engine:** English Electric 16SVT Mk2 of 1490 kW (2000 hp) at 850 rpm.
**Main Generator:** English Electric 822/4C.
**Traction Motors:** English Electric 526/5D or EE526/7D.
**Maximum Tractive Effort:** 231 kN (52000 lbf).
**Continuous Tractive Effort:** 137 kN (30900 lbf) at 18.8 mph.
**Power at Rail:** 1160 kW (1550 hp).      **Train Brakes:** Air & vacuum.
**Brake Force:** 51 t.                      **Dimensions:** 21.18 x 2.78 m.
**Weight:** 132 t.                          **Wheel Diameter:** 914/1143 mm.
**Design Speed:** 90 mph.                   **Maximum Speed:** 90 mph.
**Fuel Capacity:** 3250 litres.             **RA:** 6.
**Train Supply:** Steam.

Originally numbered D345. Currently carries the number 345.

| 40145 | **B** | 40 | ELRD | BQ |

# CLASS 43         BREL/PAXMAN         Bo-Bo

**Built:** 1975–82 by BREL at Crewe Works.
**Engine:** MTU 16V4000R41R of 1680kW (2250 hp) at 1500 rpm.
(* Paxman 12VP185 of 1565 kW (2100 hp) at 1500 rpm.)
**Main Alternator:** Brush BA1001B.
**Traction Motors:** Brush TMH68–46 or GEC G417AZ (43124–152); frame mounted.
**Maximum Tractive Effort:** 80 kN (17980 lbf).
**Continuous Tractive Effort:** 46 kN (10340 lbf) at 64.5 mph.
**Power at Rail:** 1320 kW (1770 hp).      **Train Brakes:** Air.
**Brake Force:** 35 t.                      **Dimensions:** 17.79 x 2.74 m.
**Weight:** 70.25–75.0 t.                   **Wheel Diameter:** 1020 mm.
**Design Speed:** 125 mph.                  **Maximum Speed:** 125 mph.
**Fuel Capacity:** 4500 litres.             **RA:** 5.
**Train Supply:** Three-phase electric.

† Buffer fitted.

43013, 43014 & 43062 are fitted with measuring apparatus & front-end cameras.

**Advertising liveries:**

43012 and 43126 Bristol 2015 – European Green Capital (green & white).
43144 and 43146 – Building a Greater West.
43163 – Visit Plymouth (blue).
43238 – National Railway Museum 40 Years.

| | | | | | |
|---|---|---|---|---|---|
| 43002 | **FB** | A | EFPC | LA | |
| 43003 | **FB** | A | EFPC | LA | ISAMBARD KINGDOM BRUNEL |
| 43004 | **FB** | A | EFPC | LA | First for the future/ |
| | | | | | First ar gyfer y dyfodol |
| 43005 | **FB** | A | EFPC | LA | |
| 43009 | **FB** | A | EFPC | LA | |
| 43010 | **FB** | A | EFPC | LA | |
| 43012 | **AL** | A | EFPC | LA | |
| 43013 † | **Y** | P | QCAR | EC | |
| 43014 † | **Y** | P | QCAR | EC | The Railway Observer |
| 43015 | **FB** | A | EFPC | LA | |
| 43016 | **FB** | A | EFPC | LA | |
| 43017 | **FB** | A | EFPC | LA | Hannahs discoverhannahs.org |
| 43018 | **FB** | A | EFPC | LA | |
| 43020 | **FB** | A | EFPC | LA | MTU Power. Passion. Partnership |
| 43021 | **FB** | A | EFPC | LA | David Austin – Cartoonist |
| 43022 | **FB** | A | EFPC | LA | |
| 43023 | **FB** | A | EFPC | LA | |
| 43024 | **FB** | A | EFPC | LA | Great Western Society 1961–2011 |
| | | | | | Didcot Railway Centre |
| 43025 | **FB** | A | EFPC | LA | IRO The Institution of Railway Operators |
| | | | | | 2000–2010 TEN YEARS |
| | | | | | PROMOTING OPERATIONAL EXCELLENCE |
| 43026 | **FB** | A | EFPC | LA | Michael Eavis |
| 43027 | **FB** | A | EFPC | LA | Glorious Devon |
| 43028 | **FB** | A | EFPC | LA | |
| 43029 | **FB** | A | EFPC | LA | |
| 43030 | **FB** | A | EFPC | LA | Christian Lewis Trust |
| 43031 | **FB** | A | EFPC | LA | |
| 43032 | **FB** | A | EFPC | LA | |
| 43033 | **FB** | A | EFPC | LA | Driver Brian Cooper |
| | | | | | 15 June 1947–5 October 1999 |
| 43034 | **FB** | A | EFPC | LA | TravelWatch SouthWest |
| 43035 | **FB** | A | EFPC | LA | |
| 43036 | **FB** | A | EFPC | LA | |
| 43037 | **FB** | A | EFPC | LA | PENYDARREN |
| 43040 | **FB** | A | EFPC | LA | Bristol St. Philip's Marsh |
| 43041 | **FB** | A | EFPC | LE | Meningitis Trust Support for Life |
| 43042 | **FB** | A | EFPC | LE | |
| 43043 * | **ST** | P | EMPC | NL | |
| 43044 * | **ST** | P | EMPC | NL | |
| 43045 * | **ST** | P | EMPC | NL | |
| 43046 * | **ST** | P | EMPC | NL | |
| 43047 * | **ST** | P | EMPC | NL | |
| 43048 * | **ST** | P | EMPC | NL | T.C.B. Miller MBE |

| | | | | | |
|---|---|---|---|---|---|
| 43049 * | **ST** | P | EMPC | NL | Neville Hill |
| 43050 * | **ST** | P | EMPC | NL | |
| 43052 * | **ST** | P | EMPC | NL | |
| 43053 | **FB** | P | EFPC | LE | University of Worcester |
| 43054 * | **ST** | P | EMPC | NL | |
| 43055 * | **ST** | P | EMPC | NL | The Sheffield Star 125 Years |
| 43056 | **FB** | P | EFPC | LE | The Royal British Legion |
| 43058 * | **ST** | P | EMPC | NL | |
| 43059 * | **ST** | P | EMPC | NL | |
| 43060 * | **ST** | P | EMPC | NL | |
| 43061 * | **ST** | P | EMPC | NL | |
| 43062 | **Y** | P | QCAR | EC | John Armitt |
| 43063 | **FB** | P | EFPC | LE | |
| 43064 * | **ST** | P | EMPC | NL | |
| 43066 * | **ST** | P | EMPC | NL | |
| 43069 | **FB** | P | EFPC | LE | |
| 43070 | **FB** | P | EFPC | LE | The Corps of Royal Electrical and Mechanical Engineers |
| 43071 | **FB** | P | EFPC | LE | |
| 43073 * | **ST** | P | EMPC | NL | |
| 43075 * | **ST** | P | EMPC | NL | |
| 43076 * | **ST** | P | EMPC | NL | IN SUPPORT OF HELP for HEROES |
| 43078 | **FB** | P | EFPC | LE | |
| 43079 | **FB** | P | EFPC | LE | |
| 43081 * | **ST** | P | EMPC | NL | |
| 43082 * | **ST** | P | EMPC | NL | RAILWAY children – THE VOICE FOR STREET CHILDREN WORLDWIDE |
| 43083 * | **ST** | P | EMPC | NL | |
| 43086 | **FB** | P | EFPC | OO | |
| 43087 | **FB** | P | EFPC | OO | 11 Explosive Ordnance Disposal Regiment Royal Logistic Corps |
| 43088 | **FB** | P | EFPC | OO | |
| 43089 * | **ST** | P | EMPC | NL | |
| 43091 | **FB** | P | EFPC | OO | |
| 43092 | **FB** | FG | EFPC | OO | |
| 43093 | **FB** | FG | EFPC | OO | |
| 43094 | **FB** | FG | EFPC | OO | |
| 43097 | **FB** | FG | EFPC | OO | Environment Agency |
| 43098 | **FB** | FG | EFPC | OO | |
| 43122 | **FB** | FG | EFPC | OO | |
| 43124 | **FB** | A | EFPC | LE | |
| 43125 | **FB** | A | EFPC | LE | |
| 43126 | **AL** | A | EFPC | LE | |
| 43127 | **FB** | A | EFPC | LE | Sir Peter Parker 1924–2002 Cotswold Line 150 |
| 43128 | **FB** | A | EFPC | LE | |
| 43129 | **FB** | A | EFPC | LE | |
| 43130 | **FB** | A | EFPC | LE | |
| 43131 | **FB** | A | EFPC | LE | |
| 43132 | **FB** | A | EFPC | LE | We Save the Children – Will You? |
| 43133 | **FB** | A | EFPC | LE | |

| 43134 | **FB** | A | EFPC | LE | |
| 43135 | **FB** | A | EFPC | LE | |
| 43136 | **FB** | A | EFPC | LE | |
| 43137 | **FB** | A | EFPC | LE | Newton Abbot 150 |
| 43138 | **FB** | A | EFPC | LE | |
| 43139 | **FB** | A | EFPC | LE | Driver Stan Martin ^ |
| | | | | | 25 June 1950 – 6 November 2004 |
| 43140 | **FB** | A | EFPC | LE | Landore Diesel Depot |
| | | | | | 1963 Celebrating 50 years 2013/ |
| | | | | | Depo Diesel Glandwr |
| | | | | | 1963 Dathlu 50 Mlynedd 2013 |
| 43141 | **FB** | A | EFPC | LE | |
| 43142 | **FB** | A | EFPC | LE | Reading Panel Signal Box 1965–2010 |
| 43143 | **FB** | A | EFPC | LE | Stroud 700 |
| 43144 | **AL** | A | EFPC | LE | |
| 43145 | **FB** | A | EFPC | LE | |
| 43146 | **AL** | A | EFPC | LE | |
| 43147 | **FB** | A | EFPC | LE | Royal Marines |
| | | | | | Celebrating 350 Years |
| 43148 | **FB** | A | EFPC | LE | |
| 43149 | **FB** | A | EFPC | LE | University of Plymouth |
| 43150 | **FB** | A | EFPC | LE | |
| 43151 | **FB** | A | EFPC | LE | |
| 43152 | **FB** | A | EFPC | LE | |
| 43153 | **FB** | FG | EFPC | OO | |
| 43154 | **FB** | FG | EFPC | OO | |
| 43155 | **FB** | FG | EFPC | OO | The Red Arrows |
| | | | | | 50 Seasons of Excellence |
| 43156 | **FB** | P | EFPC | OO | Dartington International Summer School |
| 43158 | **FB** | FG | EFPC | OO | |
| 43159 | **FB** | P | EFPC | OO | |
| 43160 | **FB** | P | EFPC | OO | Sir Moir Lockhead OBE |
| 43161 | **FB** | P | EFPC | OO | |
| 43162 | **FB** | P | EFPC | OO | |
| 43163 | **AL** | A | EFPC | OO | |
| 43164 | **FB** | A | EFPC | OO | |
| 43165 | **FB** | A | EFPC | OO | Prince Michael of Kent |
| 43168 | **FB** | A | EFPC | OO | |
| 43169 | **FB** | A | EFPC | OO | THE NATIONAL TRUST |
| 43170 | **FB** | A | EFPC | OO | |
| 43171 | **FB** | A | EFPC | OO | |
| 43172 | **FB** | A | EFPC | OO | |
| 43174 | **FB** | A | EFPC | OO | |
| 43175 | **FB** | A | EFPC | OO | GWR 175TH ANNIVERSARY |
| 43176 | **FB** | A | EFPC | OO | |
| 43177 | **FB** | A | EFPC | OO | |
| 43179 | **FB** | A | EFPC | OO | Pride of Laira |
| 43180 | **FB** | P | EFPC | OO | |
| 43181 | **FB** | A | EFPC | OO | |
| 43182 | **FB** | A | EFPC | OO | |
| 43183 | **FB** | A | EFPC | OO | |

| 43185 | **FB** | A | EFPC | OO | Great Western |
| 43186 | **FB** | A | EFPC | OO | |
| 43187 | **GW** | A | EFPC | OO | |
| 43188 | **GW** | A | EFPC | OO | |
| 43189 | **FB** | A | EFPC | OO | RAILWAY HERITAGE TRUST |
| 43190 | **FB** | A | EFPC | OO | |
| 43191 | **FB** | A | EFPC | OO | |
| 43192 | **FB** | A | EFPC | OO | |
| 43193 | **FB** | P | EFPC | OO | |
| 43194 | **FB** | FG | EFPC | OO | |
| 43195 | **FB** | P | EFPC | OO | |
| 43196 | **FB** | P | EFPC | OO | |
| 43197 | **FB** | P | EFPC | OO | |
| 43198 | **FB** | FG | EFPC | OO | Oxfordshire 2007 |

**Class 43/2. Rebuilt Virgin Trains East Coast, CrossCountry and Grand Central power cars.** Power cars have been renumbered by adding 200 to their original number or 400 to their original number (Grand Central), except 43123 which became 43423.

| 43206 (43006) | **EC** | A | IECP | EC | |
| 43207 (43007) | **XC** | A | EHPC | EC | |
| 43208 (43008) | **VE** | A | IECP | EC | Lincolnshire Echo |
| 43238 (43038) | **AL** | A | IECP | EC | National Railway Museum 40 Years 1975–2015 |
| 43239 (43039) | **EC** | A | IECP | EC | |
| 43251 (43051) | **VE** | A | IECP | EC | |
| 43257 (43057) | **EC** | P | IECP | EC | |
| 43272 (43072) | **EC** | P | IECP | EC | |
| 43274 (43074) | **VE** | P | IECP | EC | |
| 43277 (43077) | **EC** | P | IECP | EC | |
| 43285 (43085) | **XC** | P | EHPC | EC | |
| 43290 (43090) | **EC** | P | IECP | EC | mtu fascination of power |
| 43295 (43095) | **EC** | A | IECP | EC | |
| 43296 (43096) | **EC** | A | IECP | EC | |
| 43299 (43099) | **VE** | P | IECP | EC | |
| 43300 (43100) | **VE** | P | IECP | EC | Craigentinny 100 YEARS 1914–2014 |
| 43301 (43101) | **XC** | P | EHPC | EC | |
| 43302 (43102) | **VE** | P | IECP | EC | |
| 43303 (43103) | **XC** | P | EHPC | EC | |
| 43304 (43104) | **XC** | A | EHPC | EC | |
| 43305 (43105) | **EC** | A | IECP | EC | |
| 43306 (43106) | **EC** | A | IECP | EC | |
| 43307 (43107) | **EC** | A | IECP | EC | |
| 43308 (43108) | **VE** | A | IECP | EC | HIGHLAND CHIEFTAIN |
| 43309 (43109) | **VE** | A | IECP | EC | |
| 43310 (43110) | **VE** | A | IECP | EC | |
| 43311 (43111) | **VE** | A | IECP | EC | |
| 43312 (43112) | **VE** | A | IECP | EC | |
| 43313 (43113) | **VE** | A | IECP | EC | |
| 43314 (43114) | **EC** | A | IECP | EC | |

| | | | | | |
|---|---|---|---|---|---|
| 43315 (43115) | **EC** | A | IECP | EC | |
| 43316 (43116) | **VE** | A | IECP | EC | |
| 43317 (43117) | **VE** | A | IECP | EC | |
| 43318 (43118) | **VE** | A | IECP | EC | |
| 43319 (43119) | **VE** | A | IECP | EC | |
| 43320 (43120) | **VE** | A | IECP | EC | |
| 43321 (43121) | **XC** | P | EHPC | EC | |
| 43357 (43157) | **XC** | P | EHPC | EC | |
| 43366 (43166) | **XC** | A | EHPC | EC | |
| 43367 (43167) | **EC** | A | IECP | EC | DELTIC 50 1955–2005 |
| 43378 (43178) | **XC** | A | EHPC | EC | |
| 43384 (43184) | **XC** | A | EHPC | EC | |
| 43423 (43123) † | **GC** | A | GCHP | HT | 'VALENTA' 1972–2010 |
| 43465 (43065) † | **GC** | A | GCHP | HT | |
| 43467 (43067) † | **GC** | A | GCHP | HT | |
| 43468 (43068) † | **GC** | A | GCHP | HT | |
| 43480 (43080) † | **GC** | A | GCHP | HT | |
| 43484 (43084) † | **GC** | A | GCHP | HT | PETER FOX 1942–2011 PLATFORM 5 |

## CLASS 47                BR/BRUSH/SULZER               Co-Co

**Built:** 1963–67 by Brush Traction, at Loughborough or by BR at Crewe Works.
**Engine:** Sulzer 12LDA28C of 1920 kW (2580 hp) at 750 rpm.
**Main Generator:** Brush TG160-60 Mk4 or TM172-50 Mk1.
**Traction Motors:** Brush TM64-68 Mk1 or Mk1A.
**Maximum Tractive Effort:** 267 kN (60000 lbf).
**Continuous Tractive Effort:** 133 kN (30000 lbf) at 26 mph.
**Power at Rail:** 1550 kW (2080 hp).      **Train Brakes:** Air.
**Brake Force:** 61 t.                      **Dimensions:** 19.38 x 2.79 m.
**Weight:** 111.5–120.6 t.                  **Wheel Diameter:** 1143 mm.
**Design Speed:** 95 mph.
**Maximum Speed:** 95 mph (* 75 mph).
**Fuel Capacity:** 3273 (+ 5887).          **RA:** 6 or 7.
**Train Supply:** Not equipped.

Originally numbered in series D1100–D1111, D1500–D1999 but not in order.

Class 47s exported for use abroad are listed in section 6 of this book.

**Non-standard liveries/numbering:**

47270    Also carries the number 1971.
47773    Also carries the number D1755.
47798    Royal Train claret with Rail Express Systems markings.
47830    Also carries the number D1645.

**Class 47/0 (Dual-braked locos) or Class 47/2 (Air-braked locos). Standard Design.** Details as above.

| | | | | |
|---|---|---|---|---|
| 47194 a+ | **F** | WC | AWCX | CS (S) |
| 47236 + | **FE** | WC | AWCX | CS (S) |
| 47237 x+ | **WC** | WC | AWCA | CS |
| 47245 x+ | **WC** | WC | AWCA | CS |

47270 a+    **B**   WC AWCA      CS (S)  SWIFT

**Class 47/3 (Dual-braked locos) or Class 47/2 (Air-braked locos).**
Details as Class 47/0 except: **Weight:** 113.7 t.

| 47355 a+ | **K** | WC AWCX | CS (S) |
| 47368 x | **F** | WC AWCX | CS (S) |

**Class 47/4. Electric Train Supply equipment.**
Details as Class 47/0 except:

**Weight:** 120.4–125.1 t.                    **Fuel Capacity:** 3273 (+ 5537) litres.
**Train Supply:** Electric, index 66.         **RA:** 7.

| 47492 x | **RX** | WC AWCX | CS (S) | |
| 47500 x | **WC** | WC AWCX | CS (S) | |
| 47501 x+ | **GG** | LS MBDL | CL | |
| 47526 x | **BL** | WC AWCX | CS (S) | |
| 47580 x | **BL** | 47 MBDL | TM | County of Essex |

**Class 47/7. Former Railnet dedicated locos.** All have twin fuel tanks.

| 47727 | **CS** | CS COFS | WH | Rebecca |
| 47739 | **CS** | CS COFS | WH | Robin of Templecombe 1938–2013 |
| 47746 x | **WC** | WC AWCA | CS | Chris Fudge 29.7.70 – 22.6.10 |
| 47749 | **CS** | CS COLS | WH (S) | Demelza |
| 47760 x | **WC** | WC AWCA | CS | |
| 47768 | **RX** | WC AWCX | CS (S) | |
| 47769 | **V** | HN HNRS | BH (S) | Resolve |
| 47772 x | **RX** | WC AWCX | CS (S) | |
| 47773 x | **GG** | 70 MBDL | TM | |
| 47776 x | **RX** | WC AWCX | CS (S) | |
| 47786 | **WC** | WC AWCA | CS | Roy Castle OBE |
| 47787 | **WC** | WC AWCX | CS (S) | Windsor Castle |
| 47790 | **VN** | DR XHAC | KM | Galloway Princess |

**Class 47/4 continued.** RA6. Most fitted with extended-range fuel tanks (+).

| 47798 x | **O** | NM MBDL | YK | Prince William |
| 47802 + | **WC** | WC AWCA | CS | |
| 47804 | **WC** | WC AWCA | CS | |
| 47805 + | **DS** | DR XHAC | KM | John Scott 12.5.45–22.5.12 |
| 47810 + | **DI** | DR XHSS | CR (S) | Peter Bath MBE 1927–2006 |
| 47811 + | **GL** | FL DHLT | BA (S) | |
| 47812 + | **RB** | RV GBDF | BH | |
| 47813 + | **DS** | DR XHSS | CR (S) | Solent |
| 47815 + | **RB** | RV GBDF | BH | GREAT WESTERN |
| 47816 + | **GL** | FL DHLT | BA (S) | |
| 47818 + | **DS** | DR XHAC | KM | |
| 47826 + | **WC** | WC AWCA | CS | |
| 47828 + | **DS** | DR XHAC | KM | |
| 47830 + | **GG** | FL DFLH | LD | |
| 47832 + | **WC** | WC AWCA | CS | |
| 47841 + | **DS** | DR XHSS | ZG (S) | |
| 47843 + | **RB** | RV GBDF | BH | VULCAN |

| 47847 + | **BL** | RV | GBDF | BH    |               |
|---------|--------|----|------|-------|---------------|
| 47848 + | **RB** | RV | GBDF | BH    | TITAN STAR    |
| 47851 + | **WC** | WC | AWCA | CS    |               |
| 47853 + | **DS** | DR | XHSS | CR (S)| RAIL EXPRESS  |
| 47854 + | **WC** | WC | AWCA | CS    | Diamond Jubilee |

---

# CLASS 50          ENGLISH ELECTRIC          Co-Co

**Built:** 1967–68 by English Electric at Vulcan Foundry, Newton-le-Willows.
**Engine:** English Electric 16CVST of 2010 kW (2700 hp) at 850 rpm.
**Main Generator:** English Electric 840/4B.
**Traction Motors:** English Electric 538/5A.
**Maximum Tractive Effort:** 216 kN (48500 lbf).
**Continuous Tractive Effort:** 147 kN (33000 lbf) at 23.5 mph.

| | |
|---|---|
| **Power at Rail:** 1540 kW (2070 hp). | **Train Brakes:** Air & vacuum. |
| **Brake Force:** 59 t. | **Dimensions:** 20.88 x 2.78 m. |
| **Weight:** 116.9 t. | **Wheel Diameter:** 1092 mm. |
| **Design Speed:** 105 mph. | **Maximum Speed:** 90 mph. |
| **Fuel Capacity:** 4796 litres. | **RA:** 6. |
| **Train Supply:** Electric, index 61. | |

Originally numbered D407, D417, D444 & D449.

| 50007 | **B**  | NB | MBDL | WH | Hercules  |
|-------|--------|----|------|----|-----------|
| 50017 | **N**  | NB | MBDL | WH | Royal Oak |
| 50044 | **B**  | 50 | CFOL | KR | Exeter    |
| 50049 | **BL** | 50 | CFOL | KR | Defiance  |

---

# CLASS 52          BR/MAYBACH          C-C

**Built:** 1961–64 by BR at Swindon Works.
**Engine:** Two Maybach MD655 of 1007 kW (1350 hp) at 1500 rpm.
**Transmission:** Hydraulic. Voith L630rV.
**Maximum Tractive Effort:** 297 kN (66700 lbf).
**Continuous Tractive Effort:** 201 kN (45200 lbf) at 14.5 mph.

| | |
|---|---|
| **Power at Rail:** 1490 kW (2000 hp). | **Train Brakes:** Air & vacuum. |
| **Brake Force:** 83 t. | **Dimensions:** 20.7 m x 2.78 m. |
| **Weight:** 110 t. | **Wheel Diameter:** 1092 mm. |
| **Design Speed:** 90 mph. | **Maximum Speed:** 90 mph. |
| **Fuel Capacity:** 3900 litres. | **RA:** 6. |
| **Train Supply:** Steam. | |

Never allocated a number in the 1972 number series.

Registered on TOPS as No. 89416.

| D1015 | **M** | DT | MBDL | TM | WESTERN CHAMPION |
|-------|-------|----|------|----|------------------|

## CLASS 55          ENGLISH ELECTRIC          Co-Co

**Built:** 1961 by English Electric at Vulcan Foundry, Newton-le-Willows.
**Engine:** Two Napier-Deltic D18-25 of 1230 kW (1650 hp) each at 1500 rpm.
**Main Generators:** Two English Electric 829/1A.
**Traction Motors:** English Electric 538/A.
**Maximum Tractive Effort:** 222 kN (50000 lbf).
**Continuous Tractive Effort:** 136 kN (30500 lbf) at 32.5 mph.
**Power at Rail:** 1969 kW (2640 hp).    **Train Brakes:** Air & vacuum.
**Brake Force:** 51 t.                   **Dimensions:** 21.18 x 2.68 m.
**Weight:** 100 t.                       **Wheel Diameter:** 1092 mm.
**Design Speed:** 105 mph.               **Maximum Speed:** 100 mph.
**Fuel Capacity:** 3755 litres.          **RA:** 5.
**Train Supply:** Electric, index 66.

Originally numbered D9002, D9009 & D9000.

55022 registered on TOPS as No. 89500.

| 55002 | **B** | NM | MBDL | YK | THE KING'S OWN YORKSHIRE LIGHT INFANTRY |
| 55009 | **GG** | DP | MBDL | BH | ALYCIDON |
| 55022 | **B** | MW | MBDL | ZH | ROYAL SCOTS GREY |

## CLASS 56          BRUSH/BR/RUSTON          Co-Co

**Built:** 1976–84 by Electroputere at Craiova, Romania (as sub-contractors for Brush) or BREL at Doncaster or Crewe Works.
**Engine:** Ruston Paxman 16RK3CT of 2460 kW (3250 hp) at 900 rpm.
**Main Alternator:** Brush BA1101A.
**Traction Motors:** Brush TM73-62.
**Maximum Tractive Effort:** 275 kN (61800 lbf).
**Continuous Tractive Effort:** 240 kN (53950 lbf) at 16.8 mph.
**Power at Rail:** 1790 kW (2400 hp).    **Train Brakes:** Air.
**Brake Force:** 60 t.                   **Dimensions:** 19.36 x 2.79 m.
**Weight:** 126 t.                       **Wheel Diameter:** 1143 mm.
**Design Speed:** 80 mph.                **Maximum Speed:** 80 mph.
**Fuel Capacity:** 5228 litres.          **RA:** 7.
**Train Supply:** Not equipped.

All equipped with Slow Speed Control.

Class 56s exported for use abroad are listed in section 6 of this book.

**Non-standard liveries:**

56009 All over blue.

56081, 56098 and 56104 Unbranded Railfreight grey.

56303 All over dark green.

| 56007 | **B** | UR | UKRO | LR (S) |
| 56009 | **O** | UR | UKRS | BL (S) |
| 56018 | **FER** | UR | UKRS | LB (S) |

| | | | | |
|---|---|---|---|---|
| 56031 | **FER** | UR | UKRS | LR (S) |
| 56032 | **FER** | UR | UKRS | LR (S) |
| 56037 | **E** | UR | UKRS | BL (S) |
| 56038 | **FER** | UR | UKRS | LR (S) |
| 56049 | **CS** | CS | COLS | WH (S) |
| 56051 | **FER** | CS | COLS | WH (S) |
| 56060 | **FER** | UR | UKRS | WH (S) |
| 56065 | **FER** | UR | UKRS | LR (S) |
| 56069 | **FER** | UR | UKRS | LR (S) |
| 56077 | **LH** | UR | UKRS | BL (S) |
| 56078 | **CS** | CS | COFS | WH |
| 56081 | **O** | UR | UKRL | LR |
| 56087 | **CS** | CS | COFS | WH |
| 56090 | **FER** | CS | COLS | WH (S) |
| 56091 | **FER** | BA | HTLX | WH |
| 56094 | **CS** | CS | COFS | WH |
| 56096 | **CS** | CS | COFS | WH |
| 56098 | **O** | UR | UKRO | LR (S) |
| 56103 | **FER** | BA | HTLX | WH |
| 56104 | **O** | UR | UKRL | LR |
| 56105 | **CS** | CS | COFS | WH |
| 56106 | **FER** | UR | UKRS | LR (S) |
| 56113 | **CS** | CS | COFS | WH |
| 56128 | **F** | BA | HTLX | WH (S) |

| | | | | | |
|---|---|---|---|---|---|
| 56301 | (56045) | **FA** | 56 | HTLX | WH |
| 56302 | (56124) | **CS** | CS | COFS | WH |
| 56303 | (56125) | **O** | BA | HTLX | WH |
| 56311 | (56057) | **DC** | BA | HTLX | WH |
| 56312 | (56003) | **DC** | BA | HTLX | WH |

56312: Jeremiah Dixon Son of County Durham Surveyor of the Mason-Dixon Line U.S.A.

---

# CLASS 57        BRUSH/GM        Co-Co

**Built:** 1964–65 by Brush Traction at Loughborough or BR at Crewe Works as Class 47. Rebuilt 1997–2004 by Brush Traction at Loughborough.
**Engine:** General Motors 12 645 E3 of 1860 kW (2500 hp) at 904 rpm.
**Main Alternator:** Brush BA1101D (recovered from Class 56).
**Traction Motors:** Brush TM64-68 Mark 1 or Mark 1a.
**Maximum Tractive Effort:** 244.5 kN (55000 lbf).
**Continuous Tractive Effort:** 140 kN (31500 lbf) at ?? mph.

| | |
|---|---|
| **Power at Rail:** 1507 kW (2025 hp). | **Train Brakes:** Air. |
| **Brake Force:** 80 t. | **Dimensions:** 19.38 x 2.79 m. |
| **Weight:** 120.6 t. | **Wheel Diameter:** 1143 mm. |
| **Design Speed:** 75 mph. | **Maximum Speed:** 75 mph. |
| **Fuel Capacity:** 5550 litres. | **RA:** 6 |
| **Train Supply:** Not equipped. | |

**Non-standard livery:** 57604 – Original Great Western Railway green.

**Class 57/0. No Train Supply Equipment. Rebuilt 1997–2000.**

| | | | | | |
|---|---|---|---|---|---|
| 57001 (47356) | **WC** | WC | AWCA | CS | |
| 57002 (47322) | **DS** | P | XHCK | KM | |
| 57003 (47317) | **DI** | P | XHCK | KM | |
| 57004 (47347) | **DS** | DR | XHCK | KM | |
| 57005 (47350) | **AZ** | WC | AWCX | CS (S) | |
| 57006 (47187) | **WC** | WC | AWCX | CS (S) | |
| 57007 (47332) | **DS** | P | XHCK | KM | |
| 57008 (47060) | **DS** | P | XHCK | KM | |
| 57009 (47079) | **DS** | P | XHCK | KM | |
| 57010 (47231) | **DI** | P | XHCK | KM | |
| 57011 (47329) | **DS** | P | XHCK | KM | |
| 57012 (47204) | **DS** | P | XHCK | KM | |

**Class 57/3. Electric Train Supply Equipment. Former Virgin Trains locos. Rebuilt 2002–04.** Details as Class 57/0 except:

**Engine:** General Motors 12645F3B of 2050 kW (2750 hp) at 954 rpm.
**Main Alternator:** Brush BA1101F (recovered from a Class 56) or Brush BA1101G.
**Fuel Capacity:** 5887 litres.     **Train Supply:** Electric, index 100.
**Design Speed:** 95 mph.     **Maximum Speed:** 95 mph.
**Brake Force:** 60 t.     **Weight:** 117 t.

| | | | | | |
|---|---|---|---|---|---|
| 57301 (47845) d | **DI** | DR | XHAC | KM | Goliath |
| 57302 (47827) d | **DS** | P | XHAC | KM | Chad Varah |
| 57303 (47705) d | **DI** | DR | XHAC | KM | Pride of Carlisle |
| 57304 (47807) d | **DS** | P | XHVT | KM | Pride of Cheshire |
| 57305 (47822) d | **VN** | DR | XHAC | KM | Northern Princess |
| 57306 (47814) d | **DI** | DR | XHAC | KM | |
| 57307 (47225) d | **DR** | P | XHVT | KM | LADY PENELOPE |
| 57308 (47846) d | **DS** | P | XHVT | KM | County of Staffordshire |
| 57309 (47806) d | **DS** | P | XHVT | KM | Pride of Crewe |
| 57310 (47831) d | **DI** | DR | XHAC | KM | Pride of Cumbria |
| 57311 (47817) d | **DS** | P | XHVT | KM | Thunderbird |
| 57312 (47330) d | **VN** | DR | XHAC | KM | Solway Princess |
| 57313 (47371) | **WC** | WC | AWCA | CS | |
| 57314 (47372) | **WC** | WC | AWCA | CS | |
| 57315 (47234) | **WC** | WC | AWCA | CS | |
| 57316 (47290) | **WC** | WC | AWCA | CS | |

**Class 57/6. Electric Train Supply Equipment. Prototype ETS loco. Rebuilt 2001.** Details as Class 57/0 except:

**Main Alternator:** Brush BA1101E.     **Fuel Capacity:** 3273 litres.
**Train Supply:** Electric, index 95.     **Weight:** 113 t.
**Design Speed:** 95 mph.     **Maximum Speed:** 95 mph.
**Brake Force:** 60 t.

| | | | | | |
|---|---|---|---|---|---|
| 57601 (47825) | **WC** | WC | AWCA | CS | |

**Class 57/6. Electric Train Supply Equipment. Great Western Railway locos. Rebuilt 2004.** Details as Class 57/3.

| | | | | | |
|---|---|---|---|---|---|
| 57602 (47337) | **FB** | P | EFOO | OO | Restormel Castle |
| 57603 (47349) | **GW** | P | EFOO | OO | Tintagel Castle |
| 57604 (47209) | **O** | P | EFOO | OO | PENDENNIS CASTLE |
| 57605 (47206) | **GW** | P | EFOO | OO | Totnes Castle |

# CLASS 58         BREL/RUSTON         Co-Co

**Built:** 1983–87 by BREL at Doncaster Works.
**Engine:** Ruston Paxman 12RK3ACT of 2460 kW (3300 hp) at 1000 rpm.
**Main Alternator:** Brush BA1101B.     **Traction Motors:** Brush TM73-62.
**Maximum Tractive Effort:** 275 kN (61800 lbf).
**Continuous Tractive Effort:** 240 kN (53950 lbf) at 17.4 mph.
**Power at Rail:** 1780 kW (2387 hp).     **Train Brakes:** Air.
**Brake Force:** 60 t.                    **Dimensions:** 19.13 x 2.72 m.
**Weight:** 130 t.                        **Wheel Diameter:** 1120 mm.
**Design Speed:** 80 mph.                 **Maximum Speed:** 80 mph.
**Fuel Capacity:** 4214 litres.           **RA:** 7.
**Train Supply:** Not equipped.

All equipped with Slow Speed Control.

Class 58s exported for use abroad are listed in section 6 of this book.

| | | | | |
|---|---|---|---|---|
| 58008 | **ML** | DB | WQDA | EH (S) |
| 58012 | **F**  | DB | WQDA | TO (S) |
| 58022 | **F**  | DB | WQDA | CE (S) |
| 58023 | **ML** | DB | WQDA | TO (S) |
| 58048 | **E**  | DB | WQDA | CE (S) |

# CLASS 59         GENERAL MOTORS         Co-Co

**Built:** 1985 (59001–004) or 1989 (59005) by General Motors, La Grange, Illinois, USA or 1990 (59101–104), 1994 (59201) and 1995 (59202–206) by General Motors, London, Ontario, Canada.
**Engine:** General Motors 16-645E3C two stroke of 2460 kW (3300 hp) at 904 rpm.
**Main Alternator:** General Motors AR11 MLD-D14A.
**Traction Motors:** General Motors D77B.
**Maximum Tractive Effort:** 506 kN (113 550 lbf).
**Continuous Tractive Effort:** 291 kN (65 300 lbf) at 14.3 mph.
**Power at Rail:** 1889 kW (2533 hp).     **Train Brakes:** Air.
**Brake Force:** 69 t.                    **Dimensions:** 21.35 x 2.65 m.
**Weight:** 121 t.                        **Wheel Diameter:** 1067 mm.
**Design Speed:** 60 (* 75) mph.          **Maximum Speed:** 60 (* 75) mph.
**Fuel Capacity:** 4546 litres.           **RA:** 7.
**Train Supply:** Not equipped.

**Class 59/0. Owned by Aggregate Industries and GB Railfreight.**

| | | | | | |
|---|---|---|---|---|---|
| 59001 | **AI** | AI | XYPO | MD | YEOMAN ENDEAVOUR |
| 59002 | **AI** | AI | XYPO | MD | ALAN J DAY |
| 59003 | **GB** | GB | GBYH | PG | YEOMAN HIGHLANDER |
| 59004 | **FY** | AI | XYPO | MD | PAUL A HAMMOND |
| 59005 | **AI** | AI | XYPO | MD | KENNETH J PAINTER |

**Class 59/1. Owned by Hanson UK.**

| | | | | | |
|---|---|---|---|---|---|
| 59101 | **HA** | HA | XYPA | MD | Village of Whatley |
| 59102 | **HA** | HA | XYPA | MD | Village of Chantry |
| 59103 | **HA** | HA | XYPA | MD | Village of Mells |
| 59104 | **HA** | HA | XYPA | MD | Village of Great Elm |

**Class 59/2. Owned by DB Schenker.**

| | | | | | |
|---|---|---|---|---|---|
| 59201 | * | **DB** | DB | WDAM | MD | |
| 59202 | * | **DB** | DB | WDAM | MD | Alan Meddows Taylor MD Mendip Rail Limited |
| 59203 | * | **DB** | DB | WDAM | MD | |
| 59204 | * | **DB** | DB | WDAM | MD | |
| 59205 | *b | **DB** | DB | WDAM | MD | |
| 59206 | *b | **DB** | DB | WDAM | MD | John F. Yeoman Rail Pioneer |

# CLASS 60      BRUSH/MIRRLEES      Co-Co

**Built:** 1989–93 by Brush Traction at Loughborough.
**Engine:** Mirrlees 8MB275T of 2310 kW (3100 hp) at 1000 rpm.
**Main Alternator:** Brush BA1006A.
**Traction Motors:** Brush TM2161A.
**Maximum Tractive Effort:** 500 kN (106500 lbf).
**Continuous Tractive Effort:** 336 kN (71500 lbf) at 17.4 mph.
**Power at Rail:** 1800 kW (2415 hp).
**Brake Force:** 74 (+62) t.
**Weight:** 129 (+131) t.
**Design Speed:** 62 mph.
**Fuel Capacity:** 4546 (+ 5225) litres.
**Train Supply:** Not equipped.

**Train Brakes:** Air.
**Dimensions:** 21.34 x 2.64 m.
**Wheel Diameter:** 1118 mm.
**Maximum Speed:** 60 mph.
**RA:** 8.

All equipped with Slow Speed Control.

* Refurbished locomotives.

60034, 60064, 60072, 60073, 60077, 60084 and 60090 carry their names on one side only.

60500 originally carried the number 60016.

**Advertising liveries:** 60066 Powering Drax (silver).

60099 Tata Steel (silver).

| | | | | | |
|---|---|---|---|---|---|
| 60001 | * | **DB** | DB | WCAT | TO |
| 60002 | +* | **CS** | CS | COLO | RU |
| 60003 | + | **E** | DB | WQBA | TO (S) | FREIGHT TRANSPORT ASSOCIATION |
| 60004 | + | **E** | DB | WQBA | TO (S) |
| 60005 | + | **E** | DB | WQBA | TO (S) |
| 60006 | | **CU** | DB | WQBA | TO (S) |
| 60007 | +* | **DB** | DB | WQAA | TO (S) | The Spirit of Tom Kendell |
| 60008 | | **E** | DB | WQBA | TO (S) | Sir William McAlpine |
| 60009 | + | **E** | DB | WQBA | TO (S) |
| 60010 | +* | **DB** | DB | WCBT | TO |
| 60011 | | **DB** | DB | WCAT | TO |
| 60012 | + | **E** | DB | WQBA | TO (S) |
| 60013 | | **EG** | DB | WQCA | TO (S) | Robert Boyle |
| 60014 | | **EG** | DB | WQBA | TO (S) |
| 60015 | +* | **DB** | DB | WCBT | TO |
| 60017 | +* | **DB** | DB | WCBT | TO |
| 60018 | | **E** | DB | WQBA | TO (S) |
| 60019 | * | **DB** | DB | WCAT | TO | Port of Grimsby & Immingham |
| 60020 | +* | **DB** | DB | WCBT | TO |
| 60021 | +* | **CS** | CS | COLO | RU |
| 60022 | + | **E** | DB | WQBA | TO (S) |
| 60023 | + | **E** | DB | WQBA | TO (S) |
| 60024 | * | **DB** | DB | WCAT | TO | Clitheroe Castle |
| 60025 | + | **E** | DB | WQBA | TO (S) |
| 60026 | +* | **CS** | CS | COLO | RU |
| 60027 | + | **E** | DB | WQBA | TO (S) |
| 60028 | + | **EG** | DB | WQCA | CE (S) |
| 60029 | | **E** | DB | WQCA | CE (S) |
| 60030 | + | **E** | DB | WQBA | TO (S) |
| 60031 | | **E** | DB | WQBA | TO (S) |
| 60032 | | **F** | DB | WQBA | TO (S) |
| 60033 | + | **CU** | DB | WQCA | TO (S) | Tees Steel Express |
| 60034 | | **EG** | DB | WQBA | TO (S) | Carnedd Llewelyn |
| 60035 | | **E** | DB | WCAT | TO |
| 60036 | | **E** | DB | WQBA | TO (S) | GEFCO |
| 60037 | + | **E** | DB | WQBA | TO (S) |
| 60038 | + | **E** | DB | WQCA | CE (S) |
| 60039 | * | **DB** | DB | WCAT | TO | Dove Holes |
| 60040 | * | **DB** | DB | WCAT | TO | The Territorial Army Centenary |
| 60041 | + | **E** | DB | WQCA | TO (S) |
| 60042 | | **E** | DB | WQBA | TO (S) |
| 60043 | | **E** | DB | WQBA | TO (S) |
| 60044 | * | **DB** | DB | WCAT | TO | Dowlow |
| 60045 | | **E** | DB | WQAA | TO (S) | The Permanent Way Institution |
| 60046 | + | **EG** | DB | WQCA | CE (S) |
| 60047 | * | **CS** | CS | COLO | RU |
| 60048 | | **E** | DB | WQCA | TO (S) |
| 60049 | | **E** | DB | WCAT | TO |
| 60050 | | **E** | DB | WQBA | TO (S) |
| 60051 | + | **E** | DB | WQBA | TO (S) |

| | | | | | | |
|---|---|---|---|---|---|---|
| 60052 | +  | **E**  | DB | WQBA | TO (S) | Glofa Twr – The last deep mine in Wales – Tower Colliery |
| 60053 | | **E** | DB | WQBA | TO (S) | |
| 60054 | +* | **DB** | DB | WCBT | TO | |
| 60055 | + | **EG** | DB | WQCA | CE (S) | |
| 60056 | +* | **CS** | CS | COLO | RU | |
| 60057 | | **EG** | DB | WQBA | TO (S) | Adam Smith |
| 60058 | + | **E** | DB | WQBA | TO (S) | |
| 60059 | +* | **DB** | DB | WCBT | TO | Swinden Dalesman |
| 60060 | | **EG** | DB | WQBA | TO (S) | |
| 60061 | | **F** | DB | WQCA | TO (S) | |
| 60062 | * | **DB** | DB | WQAA | TO (S) | Stainless Pioneer |
| 60063 | * | **DB** | DB | WCAT | TO | |
| 60064 | + | **EG** | DB | WQBA | TO (S) | Back Tor |
| 60065 | | **E** | DB | WCAT | TO | Spirit of JAGUAR |
| 60066 | * | **AL** | DB | WQAA | TO (S) | |
| 60067 | | **EG** | DB | WQBA | TO (S) | |
| 60068 | | **EG** | DB | WQBA | TO (S) | |
| 60069 | | **E** | DB | WQBA | TO (S) | Slioch |
| 60070 | + | **F** | DB | WQBA | TO (S) | John Loudon McAdam |
| 60071 | + | **E** | DB | WCBT | TO | Ribblehead Viaduct |
| 60072 | | **EG** | DB | WQBA | TO (S) | Cairn Toul |
| 60073 | | **EG** | DB | WQBA | TO (S) | Cairn Gorm |
| 60074 | * | **DB** | DB | WCAT | TO | |
| 60075 | | **E** | DB | WQBA | TO (S) | |
| 60076 | * | **CS** | CS | COLO | RU | |
| 60077 | + | **EG** | DB | WQBA | TO (S) | Canisp |
| 60078 | | **ML** | DB | WQBA | TO (S) | |
| 60079 | * | **DB** | DB | WQAA | TO (S) | |
| 60080 | + | **E** | DB | WQBA | TO (S) | |
| 60081 | + | **GW** | DB | WQBA | TO (S) | |
| 60082 | | **EG** | DB | WQBA | CE (S) | |
| 60083 | | **E** | DB | WQBA | TO (S) | |
| 60084 | | **EG** | DB | WQBA | TO (S) | Cross Fell |
| 60085 | * | **CS** | CS | COLO | RU | |
| 60086 | | **EG** | DB | WQBA | TO (S) | |
| 60087 | * | **CS** | CS | COLO | RU | CLIC Sargent www.clicsargent.co.uk |
| 60088 | | **F** | DB | WQBA | TO (S) | |
| 60089 | + | **E** | DB | WQBA | TO (S) | |
| 60090 | + | **EG** | DB | WQBA | TO (S) | Quinag |
| 60091 | +* | **DB** | DB | WCBT | TO | Barry Needham |
| 60092 | +* | **DB** | DB | WCBT | TO | |
| 60093 | | **E** | DB | WQBA | TO (S) | |
| 60094 | | **E** | DB | WQBA | TO (S) | Rugby Flyer |
| 60095 | * | **CS** | CS | COLO | RU | |
| 60096 | +* | **CS** | CS | COLO | RU | |
| 60097 | + | **E** | DB | WQBA | TO (S) | |
| 60098 | + | **E** | DB | WQBA | TO (S) | |
| 60099 | | **AL** | DB | WQAA | TO (S) | |
| 60100 | * | **DB** | DB | WCAT | TO | |
| 60500 | | **E** | DB | WQBA | TO (S) | |

# CLASS 66          GENERAL MOTORS/EMD     Co-Co

**Built:** 1998–2008 by General Motors/EMD, London, Ontario, Canada (Model JT42CWR (low emission locos Model JT42CWRM)) or 2013–16 by EMD/Progress Rail, Muncie, Indiana (66752–779).
**Engine:** General Motors 12N-710G3B-EC two stroke of 2385 kW (3200 hp) at 904 rpm (low emission locos General Motors 12N-710G3B-T2).
**Main Alternator:** General Motors AR8/CA6.
**Traction Motors:** General Motors D43TR.
**Maximum Tractive Effort:** 409 kN (92000 lbf).
**Continuous Tractive Effort:** 260 kN (58390 lbf) at 15.9 mph.
**Power at Rail:** 1850 kW (2480 hp).    **Train Brakes:** Air.
**Brake Force:** 68 t.                    **Dimensions:** 21.35 x 2.64 m.
**Weight:** 127 t.                        **Wheel Diameter:** 1120 mm.
**Design Speed:** 87.5 mph.               **Maximum Speed:** 75 mph (unless stated).
**Fuel Capacity:** 6550 litres (unless stated). **RA:** 7.
**Train Supply:** Not equipped.

All equipped with Slow Speed Control.

Class 66s previously used in the UK but now in use abroad are listed in section 6 of this book. Some of the 60 DBS 66s moved to France return to Great Britain from time to time for maintenance or operational requirements.

**Advertising livery:** 66048 Stobart Rail (two tone blue & white).

**Class 66 delivery dates.** The Class 66 design and delivery has evolved over a 18-year period, with over 400 locomotives delivered. For clarity the delivery dates (by year) for each batch of locos is as follows:

| | |
|---|---|
| 66001–250 | EWS (now DB Schenker). 1998–2000 (some now in use in France or Poland). |
| 66301–305 | Fastline. 2008. Now used by DRS. |
| 66401–410 | DRS. 2003. Now in use with GB Railfreight or Colas Rail and renumbered 66733–737 and 66742–746 (66734 since scrapped). |
| 66411–420 | DRS. 2006. Now leased by Freightliner (66411/412/417 exported to Poland). |
| 66421–430 | DRS. 2007 |
| 66431–434 | DRS. 2008 |
| 66501–505 | Freightliner. 1999 |
| 66506–520 | Freightliner. 2000 |
| 66521–525 | Freightliner. 2000 (66521 since scrapped). |
| 66526–531 | Freightliner. 2001 |
| 66532–537 | Freightliner. 2001 |
| 66538–543 | Freightliner. 2001 |
| 66544–553 | Freightliner. 2001 |
| 66554 | Freightliner. 2002† |
| 66555–566 | Freightliner. 2002 |
| 66567–574 | Freightliner. 2003. 66573–574 now used by Colas Rail and renumbered 66846–847. |
| 66575–577 | Freightliner. 2004. Now used by Colas Rail and renumbered 66848–850. |
| 66578–581 | Freightliner. 2005. Now used by GBRf and renumbered 66738–741. |

| | | | | | |
|---|---|---|---|---|---|
| 66582–594 | Freightliner. 2007 (66582/583/584/586 exported to Poland). | | | | |
| 66595–599 | Freightliner. 2008 | | | | |
| 66601–606 | Freightliner. 2000 | | | | |
| 66607–612 | Freightliner. 2002 (66607/609/611/612 exported to Poland) | | | | |
| 66613–618 | Freightliner. 2003 | | | | |
| 66619–622 | Freightliner. 2005 | | | | |
| 66623–625 | Freightliner. 2007 (66624/625 exported to Poland). | | | | |
| 66701–707 | GB Railfreight. 2001 | | | | |
| 66708–712 | GB Railfreight. 2002 | | | | |
| 66713–717 | GB Railfreight. 2003 | | | | |
| 66718–722 | GB Railfreight. 2006 | | | | |
| 66723–727 | GB Railfreight. 2006 | | | | |
| 66728–732 | GB Railfreight. 2008 | | | | |
| 66747–749 | Built in 2008 as 20078968-004/006/007 (DE 6313/15/16) for Crossrail AG in the Netherlands but never used. Sold to GB Railfreight in 2012. | | | | |
| 66750–751 | Built in 2003 as 20038513-01/04 and have worked in the Netherlands, Germany and Poland. GBRf secured these two locomotives on lease in 2013. | | | | |
| 66752–772 | GB Railfreight. 2014. | | | | |
| 66773–779 | GB Railfreight. On order for delivery early 2016. | | | | |
| 66951–952 | Freightliner. 2004 | | | | |
| 66953–957 | Freightliner. 2008 | | | | |

† Replacement for 66521, written off in the Great Heck accident in 2001.

## Class 66/0. DB Schenker-operated locos.

All fitted with Swinghead Automatic "Buckeye" Combination Couplers except 66001 and 66002.

† Fitted with additional lights and drawgear for Lickey banking duties.

t Fitted with tripcocks for working over London Underground tracks between Harrow-on-the-Hill and Amersham.

| | | | | | |
|---|---|---|---|---|---|
| 66001 t | **DB** | A | WBTT | TO | |
| 66002 | E | A | WBAT | TO | |
| 66003 | E | A | WBAT | TO | |
| 66004 | E | A | WBAE | TO | |
| 66005 | E | A | WBAT | TO | |
| 66006 | E | A | WBAT | TO | |
| 66007 | E | A | WBAE | TO | |
| 66008 | E | A | WQAA | TO (S) | |
| 66009 | E | A | WBAE | TO | |
| 66011 | E | A | WBAE | TO | |
| 66012 | E | A | WBAT | TO | |
| 66013 | E | A | WQAA | TO (S) | |
| 66014 | E | A | WBAE | TO | |
| 66015 | E | A | WBAE | TO | |
| 66016 | E | A | WBAT | TO | |
| 66017 t | E | A | WBTT | TO | |
| 66018 | E | A | WBAT | TO | |
| 66019 t | E | A | WBTT | TO | |

| 66020 | E | A | WBAT | TO | | |
|-------|---|---|------|----|---|---|
| 66021 | E | A | WBAE | TO | | |
| 66023 | E | A | WBAT | TO | | |
| 66024 | E | A | WBAT | TO | | |
| 66025 | E | A | WBAE | TO | | |
| 66027 | E | A | WBAT | TO | | |
| 66030 | E | A | WBAE | TO | | |
| 66031 | E | A | WBAT | TO | | |
| 66034 | E | A | WBAT | TO | | |
| 66035 | E | A | WBAT | TO | | |
| 66037 | E | A | WBAE | TO | | |
| 66039 | E | A | WBAT | TO | | |
| 66040 | E | A | WBAT | TO | | |
| 66041 | E | A | WBAT | TO | | |
| 66043 | E | A | WBAT | TO | | |
| 66044 | E | A | WBAE | TO | | |
| 66046 | E | A | WBAE | TO | | |
| 66047 | E | A | WBAT | TO | | |
| 66048 | AL | A | WQDA | TO (S) | James the Engine |
| 66050 | E | A | WBAE | TO | EWS Energy |
| 66051 | E | A | WBAE | TO | | |
| 66053 | E | A | WBAT | TO | | |
| 66054 | E | A | WBAE | TO | | |
| 66055 † | E | A | WBLT | TO | | |
| 66056 † | E | A | WBLT | TO | | |
| 66057 † | E | A | WBLT | TO | | |
| 66058 † | DB | A | WBLT | TO | Derek Clark |
| 66059 † | E | A | WBLE | TO | | |
| 66060 | E | A | WBAT | TO | | |
| 66061 | E | A | WBAT | TO | | |
| 66063 | E | A | WBAT | TO | | |
| 66065 | E | A | WBAT | TO | | |
| 66066 | E | A | WBAT | TO | | |
| 66067 | E | A | WBAE | TO | | |
| 66068 | E | A | WBAT | TO | | |
| 66069 | E | A | WBAT | TO | | |
| 66070 | E | A | WBAT | TO | | |
| 66074 | E | A | WQAA | TO (S) | | |
| 66075 | E | A | WBAT | TO | | |
| 66076 | E | A | WBAT | TO | | |
| 66077 | E | A | WBAE | TO | Benjamin Gimbert G.C. |
| 66078 | E | A | WBAT | TO | | |
| 66079 | E | A | WBAT | TO | James Nightall G.C. |
| 66080 | E | A | WBAT | TO | | |
| 66081 | E | A | WBAT | TO | | |
| 66082 | E | A | WBAT | TO | | |
| 66083 | E | A | WBAT | TO | | |
| 66084 | E | A | WBAT | TO | | |
| 66085 | E | A | WBAE | TO | | |
| 66086 | E | A | WBAT | TO | | |
| 66087 | E | A | WBAT | TO | | |

| | | | | |
|---|---|---|---|---|
| 66088 | **E** | A | WBAT | TO |
| 66089 | **E** | A | WBAT | TO |
| 66090 | **E** | A | WBAT | TO |
| 66091 | **E** | A | WBAT | TO |
| 66092 | **E** | A | WBAE | TO |
| 66093 | **E** | A | WBAE | TO |
| 66094 | **E** | A | WBAT | TO |
| 66095 | **E** | A | WBAE | TO |
| 66096 | **E** | A | WBAE | TO |
| 66097 | **DB** | A | WBAE | TO |
| 66098 | **E** | A | WBAT | TO |
| 66099 r | **E** | A | WBBT | TO |
| 66100 r | **E** | A | WBBE | TO |
| 66101 r | **DB** | A | WBAT | TO |
| 66102 r | **E** | A | WBBE | TO |
| 66103 r | **E** | A | WQAA | TO (S) |
| 66104 r | **E** | A | WBBE | TO |
| 66105 r | **E** | A | WBBE | TO |
| 66106 r | **E** | A | WBBT | TO |
| 66107 r | **E** | A | WBBT | TO |
| 66108 r | **E** | A | WBAT | TO |
| 66109 | **E** | A | WBAT | TO |
| 66110 r | **E** | A | WBBE | TO |
| 66111 r | **E** | A | WBBT | TO |
| 66112 r | **E** | A | WBBE | TO |
| 66113 r | **E** | A | WBBT | TO |
| 66114 r | **DB** | A | WBBT | TO |
| 66115 | **E** | A | WBAT | TO |
| 66116 | **E** | A | WBAE | TO |
| 66117 | **E** | A | WBAT | TO |
| 66118 | **DB** | A | WBAE | TO |
| 66119 | **E** | A | WBAE | TO |
| 66120 | **E** | A | WBAE | TO |
| 66121 | **E** | A | WBAE | TO |
| 66122 | **E** | A | WBAE | TO |
| 66124 | **E** | A | WBAT | TO |
| 66125 | **E** | A | WBAT | TO |
| 66126 | **E** | A | WBAT | TO |
| 66127 | **E** | A | WBAT | TO |
| 66128 | **E** | A | WBAT | TO |
| 66129 | **E** | A | WBAE | TO |
| 66130 | **E** | A | WBAT | TO |
| 66131 | **E** | A | WBAT | TO |
| 66132 | **E** | A | WBAT | TO |
| 66133 | **E** | A | WBAT | TO |
| 66134 | **E** | A | WBAE | TO |
| 66135 | **E** | A | WBAE | TO |
| 66136 | **E** | A | WBAT | TO |
| 66137 | **E** | A | WBAE | TO |
| 66138 | **E** | A | WBAT | TO |
| 66139 | **E** | A | WBAT | TO |

| | | | | | |
|---|---|---|---|---|---|
| 66140 | E | A | WBAT | TO | |
| 66141 | E | A | WQAA | TO (S) | |
| 66142 | E | A | WBAT | TO | |
| 66143 | E | A | WBAT | TO | |
| 66144 | E | A | WBAT | TO | |
| 66145 | E | A | WBAT | TO | |
| 66147 | E | A | WBAT | TO | |
| 66148 | E | A | WBAT | TO | |
| 66149 | E | A | WBAE | TO | |
| 66150 | E | A | WBAT | TO | |
| 66151 | E | A | WBAE | TO | |
| 66152 | DB | A | WBAT | TO | Derek Holmes Railway Operator |
| 66154 | E | A | WBAE | TO | |
| 66155 | E | A | WBAT | TO | |
| 66156 | E | A | WBAE | TO | |
| 66158 | E | A | WBAE | TO | |
| 66160 | E | A | WBAT | TO | |
| 66161 | E | A | WBAE | TO | |
| 66162 | E | A | WBAE | TO | |
| 66164 | E | A | WBAT | TO | |
| 66165 | E | A | WBAT | TO | |
| 66167 | E | A | WQAA | LT (S) | |
| 66168 | E | A | WBAT | TO | |
| 66169 | E | A | WBAT | TO | |
| 66170 | E | A | WBAT | TO | |
| 66171 | E | A | WBAT | TO | |
| 66172 | E | A | WBAT | TO | PAUL MELLENEY |
| 66174 | E | A | WBAE | TO | |
| 66175 | E | A | WBAT | TO | |
| 66176 | E | A | WBAE | TO | |
| 66177 | E | A | WBAT | TO | |
| 66181 | E | A | WBAT | TO | |
| 66182 | E | A | WBAE | TO | |
| 66183 | E | A | WBAT | TO | |
| 66184 | E | A | WBAT | TO | |
| 66185 | DB | A | WBAT | TO | DP WORLD London Gateway |
| 66186 | E | A | WBAT | TO | |
| 66187 | E | A | WBAT | TO | |
| 66188 | E | A | WBAE | TO | |
| 66192 | E | A | WBAE | TO | |
| 66193 | E | A | WBAT | TO | |
| 66194 | E | A | WBAT | TO | |
| 66197 | E | A | WBAT | TO | |
| 66198 | E | A | WBAE | TO | |
| 66199 | E | A | WBAT | TO | |
| 66200 | E | A | WBAE | TO | |
| 66201 | E | A | WBAE | TO | |
| 66204 | E | A | WBAT | TO | |
| 66206 | E | A | WBAT | TO | |
| 66207 | E | A | WBAE | TO | |
| 66213 | E | A | WBAT | TO | |

| 66221 | **E** | A | WBAT | TO |
| 66230 | **E** | A | WBAT | TO |
| 66232 | **E** | A | WBAT | TO |
| 66238 | **E** | A | WBAE | TO |
| 66250 | **E** | A | WBAT | TO |

**Class 66/3. Former Fastline-operated loco now operated by DRS. Low emission.** Details as Class 66/0 except:

**Engine:** EMD 12N-710G3B-U2 two stroke of 2420 kW (3245 hp) at 904 rpm.
**Traction Motors:** General Motors D43TRC.
**Fuel Capacity:** 5150 litres.

| 66301 | **DS** | BN | XHIM | KM |
| 66302 | **DS** | BN | XHIM | KM |
| 66303 | **DS** | BN | XHIM | KM |
| 66304 | **DS** | BN | XHIM | KM |
| 66305 | **DS** | BN | XHIM | KM |

**66413–434. Low emission. Macquarie Group-owned.** Details as Class 66/0 except:

**Engine:** EMD 12N-710G3B-U2 two stroke of 2420 kW (3245 hp) at 904 rpm.
**Traction Motors:** General Motors D43TRC.
**Fuel Capacity:** 5150 litres.

| 66413 | **DS** | MQ | DFHG | LD |
| 66414 | **FH** | MQ | DFIN | LD |
| 66415 | **DS** | MQ | DFHG | LD |
| 66416 | **FH** | MQ | DFIN | LD |
| 66418 | **FH** | MQ | DFIN | LD |
| 66419 | **DS** | MQ | DFHG | LD |
| 66420 | **DS** | MQ | DFIN | LD |
| 66421 | **DR** | MQ | XHIM | KM |
| 66422 | **DS** | MQ | XHIM | KM |
| 66423 | **DS** | MQ | XHIM | KM |
| 66424 | **DS** | MQ | XHIM | KM |
| 66425 | **DS** | MQ | XHIM | KM |
| 66426 | **DR** | MQ | XHIM | KM |
| 66427 | **DR** | MQ | XHIM | KM |
| 66428 | **DS** | MQ | XHIM | KM |
| 66429 | **DR** | MQ | XHIM | KM |
| 66430 | **DR** | MQ | XHIM | KM |
| 66431 | **DS** | MQ | XHIM | KM |
| 66432 | **DS** | MQ | XHIM | KM |
| 66433 | **DS** | MQ | XHIM | KM |
| 66434 | **DR** | MQ | XHIM | KM |

**Class 66/5. Freightliner-operated locos.** Details as Class 66/0.

**Advertising livery:** 66522 Shanks Waste (one half of loco Freightliner green and one half Shanks' Waste light green).

| 66501 | **FL** | P | DFIM | LD | Japan 2001 |
| 66502 | **FL** | P | DFIM | LD | Basford Hall Centenary 2001 |

| | | | | | |
|---|---|---|---|---|---|
| 66503 | FL | P | DFIM | LD | The RAILWAY MAGAZINE |
| 66504 | FH | P | DFIM | LD | |
| 66505 | FL | P | DFIM | LD | |
| 66506 | FL | E | DFHH | LD | Crewe Regeneration |
| 66507 | FL | E | DFHH | LD | |
| 66508 | FL | E | DFHH | LD | |
| 66509 | FL | E | DFHH | LD | |
| 66510 | FL | E | DFHH | LD | |
| 66511 | FL | E | DFHH | LD | |
| 66512 | FL | E | DFHH | LD | |
| 66513 | FL | E | DFHH | LD | |
| 66514 | FL | E | DFHH | LD | |
| 66515 | FL | E | DFHH | LD | |
| 66516 | FL | E | DFIM | LD | |
| 66517 | FL | E | DFHH | LD | |
| 66518 | FL | E | DFHH | LD | |
| 66519 | FL | E | DFHH | LD | |
| 66520 | FL | E | DFHH | LD | |
| 66522 | AL | E | DFHH | LD | |
| 66523 | FL | E | DFHH | LD | |
| 66524 | FL | E | DFHH | LD | |
| 66525 | FL | E | DFHH | LD | |
| 66526 | FL | P | DFHH | LD | Driver Steve Dunn (George) |
| 66527 | FL | P | DFHH | LD | Don Raider |
| 66528 | FH | P | DFHH | LD | Madge Elliot MBE |
| | | | | | Borders Railway Opening 2015 |
| 66529 | FL | P | DFHH | LD | |
| 66530 | FL | P | DFHH | LD | |
| 66531 | FL | P | DFHH | LD | |
| 66532 | FL | P | DFIM | LD | P&O Nedlloyd Atlas |
| 66533 | FL | P | DFIM | LD | Hanjin Express/Senator Express |
| 66534 | FL | P | DFIM | LD | OOCL Express |
| 66535 | FL | P | DFHH | LD | |
| 66536 | FL | P | DFHH | LD | |
| 66537 | FL | P | DFIM | LD | |
| 66538 | FL | E | DFIM | LD | |
| 66539 | FL | E | DFHH | LD | |
| 66540 | FL | E | DFIM | LD | Ruby |
| 66541 | FL | E | DFIM | LD | |
| 66542 | FL | E | DFIM | LD | |
| 66543 | FL | E | DFHH | LD | |
| 66544 | FL | P | DFHH | LD | |
| 66545 | FL | P | DFHH | LD | |
| 66546 | FL | P | DFHH | LD | |
| 66547 | FL | P | DFHH | LD | |
| 66548 | FL | P | DFHH | LD | |
| 66549 | FL | P | DFHH | LD | |
| 66550 | FL | P | DFHH | LD | |
| 66551 | FL | P | DFHH | LD | |
| 66552 | FL | P | DFHH | LD | Maltby Raider |
| 66553 | FL | P | DFHH | LD | |

| 66554 | FL | E | DFHH | LD | |
| 66555 | FL | E | DFHH | LD | |
| 66556 | FL | E | DFIM | LD | |
| 66557 | FL | E | DFHH | LD | |
| 66558 | FL | E | DFIM | LD | |
| 66559 | FL | E | DFHH | LD | |
| 66560 | FL | E | DFHH | LD | |
| 66561 | FL | E | DFHH | LD | |
| 66562 | FL | E | DFHH | LD | |
| 66563 | FL | E | DFHH | LD | |
| 66564 | FL | E | DFHH | LD | |
| 66565 | FL | E | DFHH | LD | |
| 66566 | FL | E | DFIM | LD | |
| 66567 | FL | E | DFIM | LD | |
| 66568 | FL | E | DFIM | LD | |
| 66569 | FL | E | DFIM | LD | |
| 66570 | FL | E | DFIM | LD | |
| 66571 | FL | E | DFIM | LD | |
| 66572 | FL | E | DFIM | LD | |

**Class 66/5. Freightliner-operated low emission locos.** Details as Class 66/0 except:

**Engine:** EMD 12N-710G3B-U2 two stroke of 2420 kW (3245 hp) at 904 rpm.
**Traction Motors:** General Motors D43TRC.
**Fuel Capacity:** 5150 litres.

| 66585 | FL | MQ | DFHG | LD | The Drax Flyer |
| 66587 | FL | MQ | DFIN | LD | |
| 66588 | FL | MQ | DFIN | LD | |
| 66589 | FL | MQ | DFIN | LD | |
| 66590 | FL | MQ | DFIN | LD | |
| 66591 | FL | MQ | DFIN | LD | |
| 66592 | FL | MQ | DFIN | LD | Johnson Stevens Agencies |
| 66593 | FL | MQ | DFIN | LD | 3MG MERSEY MULTIMODAL GATEWAY |
| 66594 | FL | MQ | DFIN | LD | NYK Spirit of Kyoto |
| 66595 | FL | BN | DFHG | LD | |
| 66596 | FL | BN | DFHG | LD | |
| 66597 | FL | BN | DFHG | LD | Viridor |
| 66598 | FL | BN | DFHG | LD | |
| 66599 | FL | BN | DFHG | LD | |

**Class 66/6. Freightliner-operated locomotives with modified gear ratios.** Details as Class 66/0 except:

**Maximum Tractive Effort:** 467 kN (105080 lbf).
**Continuous Tractive Effort:** 296 kN (66630 lbf) at 14.0 mph.
**Design Speed:** 65 mph.                **Maximum Speed:** 65 mph.

| 66601 | FL | P | DFHH | LD | The Hope Valley |
| 66602 | FL | P | DFHH | LD | |
| 66603 | FL | P | DFHH | LD | |
| 66604 | FL | P | DFHH | LD | |
| 66605 | FL | P | DFHH | LD | |

| | | | | | |
|---|---|---|---|---|---|
| 66606 | **FL** | P | DFHH | LD | |
| 66607 | **FL** | P | DFHH | LD | |
| 66610 | **FL** | P | DFHH | LD | |
| 66613 | **FL** | E | DFHH | LD | |
| 66614 | **FL** | E | DFHH | LD | |
| 66615 | **FL** | E | DFHH | LD | |
| 66616 | **FL** | E | DFHH | LD | |
| 66617 | **FL** | E | DFHH | LD | |
| 66618 | **FL** | E | DFHH | LD | Railways Illustrated Annual Photographic Awards Alan Barnes Derek W. Johnson MBE |
| 66619 | **FL** | E | DFHH | LD | |
| 66620 | **FL** | E | DFHH | LD | |
| 66621 | **FL** | E | DFHH | LD | |
| 66622 | **FL** | E | DFHH | LD | |

**Class 66/6. Freightliner-operated low emission loco with modified gear ratios. Fuel Capacity: 5150 litres.**

**Non-standard livery:** 66623 Bardon Aggregates blue.

| | | | | | |
|---|---|---|---|---|---|
| 66623 | **0** | MQ | DFHG | LD | Bill Bolsover |

**Class 66/7. GB Railfreight-operated locos. Details as Class 66/0.**

**Non-standard/advertising liveries:**

66709 MSC – blue with images of a container ship.

66718 London Underground 150, (black).

66720 Day and night (various colours, different on each side).

66721 London Underground 150 (white with tube map images).

| | | | | | |
|---|---|---|---|---|---|
| 66701 | **GB** | E | GBCM | RR | |
| 66702 | **GB** | E | GBCM | RR | Blue Lightning |
| 66703 | **GB** | E | GBCM | RR | Doncaster PSB 1981–2002 |
| 66704 | **GB** | E | GBCM | RR | Colchester Power Signalbox |
| 66705 | **GB** | E | GBCM | RR | Golden Jubilee |
| 66706 | **GB** | E | GBCM | RR | Nene Valley |
| 66707 | **GB** | E | GBCM | RR | Sir Sam Fay GREAT CENTRAL RAILWAY |
| 66708 | **GB** | E | GBCM | RR | Jayne |
| 66709 | **AL** | E | GBCM | RR | Sorrento |
| 66710 | **GB** | E | GBCM | RR | Phil Packer BRIT |
| 66711 | **AI** | E | GBCM | RR | Sence |
| 66712 | **GB** | E | GBCM | RR | Peterborough Power Signalbox |
| 66713 | **GB** | E | GBCM | RR | Forest City |
| 66714 | **GB** | E | GBCM | RR | Cromer Lifeboat |
| 66715 | **GB** | E | GBCM | RR | VALOUR – IN MEMORY OF ALL RAILWAY EMPLOYEES WHO GAVE THEIR LIVES FOR THEIR COUNTRY |
| 66716 | **GB** | E | GBCM | RR | LOCOMOTIVE & CARRIAGE INSTITUTION CENTENARY 1911–2011 |
| 66717 | **GB** | E | GBCM | RR | Good Old Boy |

**66718–746. Low emission. GB Railfreight locos.** 66733–737 renumbered from former DRS locos 66401–405. 66738–741 renumbered from former Freightliner locos 66578–581. 66742–746 renumbered from former DRS/Colas Rail locos 66406–410/841–845.

All details as Class 66/0 except 66718–732/747–749 as below:

**Engine:** EMD 12N-710G3B-U2 two stroke of 2420 kW (3245 hp) at 904 rpm.
**Traction Motors:** General Motors D43TRC.
**Fuel Capacity:** 5546 litres (66718–722) or 5150 litres (66723–732/747–749).

66747–749 were originally built for Crossrail AG in the Netherlands.

66750/751 were built for mainland Europe in 2003.

| | | | | | |
|---|---|---|---|---|---|
| 66718 | **AL** | E | GBCM | RR | Sir Peter Hendy CBE |
| 66719 | **GB** | E | GBCM | RR | METRO-LAND |
| 66720 | **O** | E | GBCM | RR | |
| 66721 | **AL** | E | GBCM | RR | Harry Beck |
| 66722 | **GB** | E | GBCM | RR | Sir Edward Watkin |
| 66723 | **FS** | E | GBSD | RR | Chinook |
| 66724 | **FS** | E | GBSD | RR | Drax Power Station |
| 66725 | **FS** | E | GBSD | RR | SUNDERLAND |
| 66726 | **FS** | E | GBSD | RR | SHEFFIELD WEDNESDAY |
| 66727 | **FS** | E | GBSD | RR | Andrew Scott CBE |
| 66728 | **GB** | P | GBCM | RR | Institution of Railway Operators |
| 66729 | **GB** | P | GBCM | RR | DERBY COUNTY |
| 66730 | **GB** | P | GBCM | RR | Whitemoor |
| 66731 | **GB** | P | GBCM | RR | interhub GB |
| 66732 | **GB** | P | GBCM | RR | GBRf The First Decade 1999–2009 John Smith – MD |

| | | | | | | |
|---|---|---|---|---|---|---|
| 66733 | (66401) r | **GB** | P | GBFM | RR | Cambridge PSB |
| 66735 | (66403) r | **GB** | P | GBFM | RR | |
| 66736 | (66404) r | **GB** | P | GBFM | RR | WOLVERHAMPTON WANDERERS |
| 66737 | (66405) r | **GB** | P | GBFM | RR | Lesia |
| 66738 | (66578) | **GB** | BN | GBCM | RR | HUDDERSFIELD TOWN |
| 66739 | (66579) | **GB** | BN | GBCM | RR | Bluebell Railway |
| 66740 | (66580) | **GB** | BN | GBCM | RR | Sarah |
| 66741 | (66581) | **GB** | BN | GBCM | RR | Swanage Railway |
| 66742 | (66406, 66841) | **GB** | BN | GBRT | RR | ABP Port of Immingham Centenary 1912–2012 |
| 66743 | (66407, 66842) | **GB** | BN | GBRT | RR | |
| 66744 | (66408, 66843) | **GB** | BN | GBRT | RR | Crossrail |
| 66745 | (66409, 66844) | **GB** | BN | GBRT | RR | Modern Railways The first 50 years |
| 66746 | (66410, 66845) | **GB** | BN | GBRT | RR | |
| 66747 | (20078968-007) | **U** | GB | GBNL | RR | |
| 66748 | (20078968-004) | **U** | GB | GBNL | RR | |
| 66749 | (20078968-003) | **U** | GB | GBNL | RR | |
| 66750 | (20038513-01) | **GB** | BN | GBDR | RR | Bristol Panel Signal Box |
| 66751 | (20038513-04) c | **GB** | BN | GBDR | RR | Inspirational Delivered Hitachi Rail Europe |

**66752–779. Low emission.** New build locomotives (66773–779 on order).

**Engine:** EMD 12N-710G3B-U2 two stroke of 2420 kW (3245 hp) at 904 rpm.
**Traction Motors:** General Motors D43TRC.
**Fuel Capacity:** 5150 litres.

| | | | | | |
|---|---|---|---|---|---|
| 66752 | **GB** | GB | GBNB | RR | The Hoosier State |
| 66753 | **GB** | GB | GBNB | RR | EMD Roberts Road |
| 66754 | **GB** | GB | GBNB | RR | Northampton Saints |
| 66755 | **GB** | GB | GBNB | RR | |
| 66756 | **GB** | GB | GBNB | RR | |
| 66757 | **GB** | GB | GBNB | RR | West Somerset Railway |
| 66758 | **GB** | GB | GBNB | RR | |
| 66759 | **GB** | GB | GBNB | RR | Chippy |
| 66760 | **GB** | GB | GBNB | RR | |
| 66761 | **GB** | GB | GBNB | RR | Wensleydale Railway Association 25 Years 1990–2015 |
| 66762 | **GB** | GB | GBNB | RR | |
| 66763 | **GB** | GB | GBNB | RR | |
| 66764 | **GB** | GB | GBNB | RR | |
| 66765 | **GB** | GB | GBNB | RR | |
| 66766 | **GB** | GB | GBNB | RR | |
| 66767 | **GB** | GB | GBNB | RR | |
| 66768 | **GB** | GB | GBNB | RR | |
| 66769 | **GB** | GB | GBNB | RR | |
| 66770 | **GB** | GB | GBNB | RR | |
| 66771 | **GB** | GB | GBNB | RR | |
| 66772 | **GB** | GB | GBNB | RR | |
| 66773 | | | | | |
| 66774 | | | | | |
| 66775 | | | | | |
| 66776 | | | | | |
| 66777 | | | | | |
| 66778 | | | | | |
| 66779 | | | | | |

**Class 66/8. Colas Rail locos.** Renumbered from former Freightliner locos 66573–577. Details as Class 66/0.

| | | | | | |
|---|---|---|---|---|---|
| 66846 (66573) | **CS** | CS | COLO | RU | |
| 66847 (66574) | **CS** | CS | COLO | RU | |
| 66848 (66575) | **CS** | CS | COLO | RU | |
| 66849 (66576) | **CS** | CS | COLO | RU | Wylam Dilly |
| 66850 (66577) | **CS** | CS | COLO | RU | David Maidment OBE |

**Class 66/9. Freightliner locos. Low emission "demonstrator" locos.** Details as Class 66/0 except:

**Engine:** EMD 12N-710G3B-U2 two stroke of 2420 kW (3245 hp) at 904 rpm.
**Traction Motors:** General Motors D43TRC.
**Fuel Capacity:** 5905/5150 litres.

| | | | | |
|---|---|---|---|---|
| 66951 | **FL** | E | DFHG | LD |
| 66952 | **FL** | E | DFHG | LD |

**Class 66/9. Freightliner-operated low emission locos.** Owing to the 665xx number range being full, subsequent deliveries of 66/5s were numbered from 66953 onwards. Details as Class 66/5 (low emission).

| | | | | | |
|---|---|---|---|---|---|
| 66953 | **FL** | BN | DFHG | LD | |
| 66954 | **FL** | BN | DFIN | LD | |
| 66955 | **FL** | BN | DFIN | LD | |
| 66956 | **FL** | BN | DFHG | LD | |
| 66957 | **FL** | BN | DFHG | LD | Stephenson Locomotive Society 1909–2009 |

# CLASS 67    ALSTOM/GENERAL MOTORS EMD Bo-Bo

**Built:** 1999–2000 by Alstom at Valencia, Spain, as sub-contractors for General Motors (General Motors model JT42 HW-HS).
**Engine:** GM 12N-710G3B-EC two stroke of 2385 kW (3200 hp) at 904 rpm.
**Main Alternator:** General Motors AR9A/HEP7/CA6C.
**Traction Motors:** General Motors D43FM.
**Maximum Tractive Effort:** 141 kN (31770 lbf).
**Continuous Tractive Effort:** 90 kN (20200 lbf) at 46.5 mph.

| | |
|---|---|
| **Power at Rail:** 1860 kW. | **Train Brakes:** Air. |
| **Brake Force:** 78 t. | **Dimensions:** 19.74 x 2.72 m. |
| **Weight:** 90 t. | **Wheel Diameter:** 965 mm. |
| **Design Speed:** 125 mph. | **Maximum Speed:** 125 mph. |
| **Fuel Capacity:** 4927 litres. | **RA:** 8. |
| **Train Supply:** Electric, index 66. | |

All equipped with Slow Speed Control and Swinghead Automatic "Buckeye" Combination Couplers.

67001/002/003/014/022/029 have been modified to operate in push-pull mode on the Arriva Trains Wales loco-hauled sets.

67004, 67007, 67009 and 67011 are fitted with cast iron brake blocks for working the Fort William Sleeper. **Maximum Speed:** 80 mph.

**Non-standard liveries:**

67026 Diamond Jubilee silver.

67029 All over silver with DB logos.

| | | | | |
|---|---|---|---|---|
| 67001 | **AB** | A | WAWC | CE |
| 67002 | **AB** | A | WQAA | CE (S) |
| 67003 | **AB** | A | WAAC | CE |
| 67004 r | **CA** | A | WABC | CE       Cairn Gorm |
| 67005 | **RZ** | A | WAAC | CE       Queen's Messenger |
| 67006 | **RZ** | A | WAAC | CE       Royal Sovereign |
| 67007 r | **E** | A | WABC | CE |
| 67008 | **E** | A | WAAC | CE |
| 67009 r | **E** | A | WABC | CE |

| 67010 | CA | A | WAAC | CE | |
| 67011 r | E | A | WABC | CE | |
| 67012 | CM | A | WAAC | CE | |
| 67013 | DB | A | WAAC | CE | |
| 67014 | CM | A | WAWC | CE | |
| 67015 | DB | A | WAAC | CE | |
| 67016 | E | A | WAAC | CE | |
| 67017 | E | A | WAAC | CE | Arrow |
| 67018 | DB | A | WAAC | CE | Keith Heller |
| 67019 | E | A | WQAA | TO (S) | |
| 67020 | E | A | WAAC | CE | |
| 67021 | E | A | WAAC | CE | |
| 67022 | E | A | WAAC | CE | |
| 67023 | E | A | WAAC | CE | |
| 67024 | E | A | WAAC | CE | |
| 67025 | E | A | WQAA | CE (S) | Western Star |
| 67026 | 0 | A | WAAC | CE | Diamond Jubilee |
| 67027 | DB | A | WQAA | CE (S) | |
| 67028 | E | A | WAAC | CE | |
| 67029 | 0 | A | WAWC | CE | Royal Diamond |
| 67030 r | E | A | WABC | CE | |

# CLASS 68            VOSSLOH            Bo-Bo

New Vossloh mixed-traffic locos currently being delivered to DRS. 68015–032 are under construction.

**Built:** 2012–16 by Vossloh, Valencia, Spain.
**Engine:** Caterpillar C175-16 of 2800 kW (3750 hp) at 1740 rpm.
**Main Alternator:** ABB WGX560.
**Traction Motors:** 4 x AC frame mounted ABB 4FRA6063.
**Maximum Tractive Effort:** 317 kN (71 260 lbf).
**Continuous Tractive Effort:**
**Power at Rail:**                          **Train Brakes:** Air.
**Brake Force:** 73 t.                       **Dimensions:** 20.50 x 2.69 m.
**Weight:** 85 t.                            **Wheel Diameter:** 1100 mm.
**Design Speed:** 100 mph.                   **Maximum Speed:** 100 mph.
**Fuel Capacity:** 6000 litres.              **RA:** 7.
**Train Supply:** Electric, index 96.

68010–015 have been modified to operate in push-pull mode on the Chiltern Railways loco-hauled sets.

| 68001 | DI | BN | XHVE | CR | Evolution |
| 68002 | DI | BN | XHVE | CR | Intrepid |
| 68003 | DI | BN | XHVE | CR | Astute |
| 68004 | DI | BN | XHVE | CR | Rapid |
| 68005 | DI | BN | XHVE | CR | Defiant |
| 68006 | SR | BN | XHVE | CR | Daring |
| 68007 | SR | BN | XHVE | CR | Valiant |
| 68008 | DI | BN | XHVE | CR | Avenger |

| 68009 | **DI** | BN | XHVE | CR | Titan |
|-------|--------|----|------|----|-------|
| 68010 | **CM** | BN | XHCE | CR | |
| 68011 | **CM** | BN | XHCE | CR | |
| 68012 | **CM** | BN | XHCE | CR | |
| 68013 | **CM** | BN | XHCE | CR | |
| 68014 | **CM** | BN | XHCE | CR | |
| 68015 | **CM** | BN | XHCE | CR | |
| 68016 | | BN | | | |
| 68017 | | BN | | | |
| 68018 | | BN | | | |
| 68019 | | BN | | | |
| 68020 | | BN | | | |
| 68021 | | BN | | | |
| 68022 | | BN | | | |
| 68023 | | BN | | | |
| 68024 | | BN | | | |
| 68025 | | BN | | | |
| 68026 | | BN | | | |
| 68027 | | BN | | | |
| 68028 | | BN | | | |
| 68029 | | BN | | | |
| 68030 | | BN | | | |
| 68031 | | BN | | | |
| 68032 | | BN | | | |

# CLASS 70        GENERAL ELECTRIC        Co-Co

New GE "PowerHaul" locomotives. 70012 was badly damaged whilst being unloaded in 2011 and was returned to Pennsylvania.

70801 (built as 70099) is a Turkish-built demonstrator that arrived in Britain in October 2012. Colas Rail leased this locomotive and then in 2013 ordered a further nine locomotives (70802–810) that were delivered in 2014.

**Built:** 2009–14 by General Electric, Erie, Pennsylvania, USA or by TÜLOMSAS, Eskişehir, Turkey (70801).
**Engine:** General Electric PowerHaul P616LDA1 of 2848 kW (3820 hp) at 1500 rpm.
**Main Alternator:** General Electric GTA series.
**Traction Motors:** AC-GE 5GEB30.
**Maximum Tractive Effort:** 544 kN (122 000 lbf).
**Continuous Tractive Effort:** 427 kN (96000 lbf) at ?? m.p.h.

| | |
|---|---|
| **Power at Rail:** | **Train Brakes:** Air. |
| **Brake Force:** 96.7 t. | **Dimensions:** 21.71 x 2.64 m. |
| **Weight:** 129 t. | **Wheel Diameter:** 1066 mm. |
| **Design Speed:** 75 mph. | **Maximum Speed:** 75 mph. |
| **Fuel Capacity:** 6000 litres. | **RA:** 7. |
| **Train Supply:** Not equipped. | |

## Class 70/0. Freightliner locomotives.

| 70001 | **FH** | MQ | DFGI | LD | PowerHaul |
| 70002 | **FH** | MQ | DFGI | LD | |
| 70003 | **FH** | MQ | DFGH | LD | |
| 70004 | **FH** | MQ | DFGH | LD | The Coal Industry Society |
| 70005 | **FH** | MQ | DFGH | LD | |
| 70006 | **FH** | MQ | DFGI | LD | |
| 70007 | **FH** | MQ | DFGI | LD | |
| 70008 | **FH** | MQ | DFGI | LD | |
| 70009 | **FH** | MQ | DFGI | LD | |
| 70010 | **FH** | MQ | DFGI | LD | |
| 70011 | **FH** | MQ | DFGI | LD | |
| 70013 | **FH** | MQ | DFGI | LD | |
| 70014 | **FH** | MQ | DFGI | LD | |
| 70015 | **FH** | MQ | DFGI | LD | |
| 70016 | **FH** | MQ | DFGI | LD | |
| 70017 | **FH** | MQ | DFGI | LD | |
| 70018 | **FH** | MQ | DFGI | LD | |
| 70019 | **FH** | MQ | DFGI | LD | |
| 70020 | **FH** | MQ | DFGI | LD | |

## Class 70/8. Colas Rail locomotives.

| 70801 | **CS** | LF | COLO | RU |
| 70802 | **CS** | LF | COLO | RU |
| 70803 | **CS** | LF | COLO | RU |
| 70804 | **CS** | LF | COLO | RU |
| 70805 | **CS** | LF | COLO | RU |
| 70806 | **CS** | LF | COLO | RU |
| 70807 | **CS** | LF | COLO | RU |
| 70808 | **CS** | LF | COLO | RU |
| 70809 | **CS** | LF | COLO | RU |
| 70810 | **CS** | LF | COLO | RU |

# 2. ELECTRO-DIESEL & ELECTRIC LOCOMOTIVES

## CLASS 73/1          BR/ENGLISH ELECTRIC          Bo-Bo

Electro-diesel locomotives which can operate either from a DC supply or using power from a diesel engine.

**Built:** 1965–67 by English Electric Co. at Vulcan Foundry, Newton-le-Willows.
**Engine:** English Electric 4SRKT of 447 kW (600 hp) at 850 rpm.
**Main Generator:** English Electric 824/5D.
**Electric Supply System:** 750 V DC from third rail.
**Traction Motors:** English Electric 546/1B.
**Maximum Tractive Effort (Electric):** 179 kN (40000 lbf).
**Maximum Tractive Effort (Diesel):** 160 kN (36000 lbf).
**Continuous Rating (Electric):** 1060 kW (1420 hp) giving a tractive effort of 35 kN (7800 lbf) at 68 mph.
**Continuous Tractive Effort (Diesel):** 60 kN (13600 lbf) at 11.5 mph.
**Maximum Rail Power (Electric):** 2350 kW (3150 hp) at 42 mph.
**Train Brakes:** Air, vacuum & electro-pneumatic († Air & electro-pneumatic).
**Brake Force:** 31 t.                    **Dimensions:** 16.36 x 2.64 m.
**Weight:** 77 t.                         **Wheel Diameter:** 1016 mm.
**Design Speed:** 90 mph.                 **Maximum Speed:** 90 mph.
**Fuel Capacity:** 1409 litres.          **RA:** 6.
**Train Supply:** Electric, index 66 (on electric power only).

Formerly numbered E6001–E6020/E6022–E6026/E6028–E6049 (not in order).

Locomotives numbered in the 732xx series are classed as 73/2 and were originally dedicated to Gatwick Express services.

Two separate rebuild projects are underway. For GBRf at least 11 locomotives are being rebuilt at Brush, Loughborough with a 1600 hp MTU engine (these are being renumbered in the 73961 onwards series). For Network Rail 73104/211 are being rebuilt at RVEL, Derby with a pair of QSK19 750 hp engines (these have been renumbered 73951/952).

**Non-standard liveries:**

73128 Two-tone grey.
73139 Weardale Railway brown & cream.

| 73101 | **PC** | RE | RVLO | ZA (S) | |
| 73107 | **GB** | GB | GBED | SE | Tracy |
| 73109 | **GB** | GB | GBED | SE | |
| 73119 | **GB** | GB | GBED | SE | Borough of Eastleigh |
| 73128 | **0** | GB | GBED | SE | OVS Bulleid CBE |
| 73133 | **TT** | TT | MBED | BM | |
| 73134 | **IC** | GB | GBBR | LB (S) | Woking Homes 1885–1985 |
| 73136 | **GB** | GB | GBED | SE | Mhairi |
| 73138 | **Y** | NR | QADD | ZA | |

| 73139 |   | **O** | RE | RVLO | ZA (S) |           |
|-------|---|-------|----|------|--------|-----------|
| 73141 |   | **GB** | GB | GBED | SE | Charlotte |
| 73201 | † | **B** | GB | GBED | SE | Broadlands |
| 73202 | † | **SN** | P | MBED | SL |           |
| 73212 | † | **GB** | GB | GBED | SE | Fiona     |
| 73213 | † | **GB** | GB | GBED | SE | Rhodalyn  |
| 73235 | † | **SD** | P | HYWD | BM |           |

## CLASS 73/9 (RVEL)    BR/RVEL                    Bo-Bo

The 7395x number series is reserved for rebuilt Network Rail locomotives.

**Rebuilt:** Re-engineered by RVEL Derby 2013–15.
**Engine:** 2 x QSK19 of 560 kW (750 hp) at 1800 rpm (total 1120 kw (1500 hp)).
**Main Alternator:** 2 x Marathon Magnaplus.
**Electric Supply System:** 750 V DC from third rail.
**Traction Motors:** English Electric 546/1B.
**Maximum Tractive Effort (Electric):** 179 kN (40000 lbf).
**Maximum Tractive Effort (Diesel):** 179 kN (40000 lbf).
**Continuous Rating (Electric):** 1060 kW (1420 hp) giving a tractive effort of 35 kN (7800 lbf) at 68 mph.
**Continuous Tractive Effort (Diesel):** 990 kW (1328 hp) giving a tractive effort of 33 kN (7420 lbf) at 68 mph.
**Maximum Rail Power (Electric):** 2350 kW (3150 hp) at 42 mph.

| | |
|---|---|
| **Train Brakes:** Air. | **Brake Force:** 31 t. |
| **Weight:** 77 t. | **Dimensions:** 16.36 x 2.64 m. |
| **Maximum Speed:** 90 mph. | **Wheel Diameter:** 1016 mm. |
| **Fuel Capacity:** 2260 litres. | **RA:** 6. |
| **Train Supply:** None. | |

| 73951 | (73104) | **Y** | RE | QADD | ZA |
|-------|---------|-------|----|------|----|
| 73952 | (73211) | **Y** | RE | QADD | ZA |

## CLASS 73/9 (GBRf)    BR/BRUSH                    Bo-Bo

GBRf Class 73s are being rebuilt at Brush Loughborough. 73961–965 are used on Network Rail contracts whilst 73966–971 are being rebuilt for use on the Caledonian Sleeper contract.

**Rebuilt:** Re-engineered by Brush, Loughborough 2014– .
**Engine:** MTU 8V4000 R43L of 1195 kW (1600 hp) at 1800 rpm.
**Main Alternator:** Lechmotoren SDV 87.53-12.
**Electric Supply System:** 750 V DC from third rail (73961–965 only).
**Traction Motors:** English Electric 546/1B.
**Maximum Tractive Effort (Electric):** 179 kN (40000 lbf).
**Maximum Tractive Effort (Diesel):** 179 kN (40000 lbf).
**Continuous Rating (Electric):** 1060 kW (1420 hp) giving a tractive effort of 35 kN (7800 lbf) at 68 mph.
**Continuous Tractive Effort (Diesel):** awaited.
**Maximum Rail Power (Electric):** 2350 kW (3150 hp) at 42 mph.

| | |
|---|---|
| **Train Brakes:** Air. | **Brake Force:** 31 t. |
| **Weight:** 77 t. | **Dimensions:** 16.36 x 2.64 m. |

**Maximum Speed:** 90 mph.          **Wheel Diameter:** 1016 mm.
**Fuel Capacity:** 1409 litres.          **RA:** 6.
**Train Supply:** Electric, index 38 (electric & diesel).

| | | | | | |
|---|---|---|---|---|---|
| 73961 | (73209) | **GB** | GB | GBNR | SE | Alison |
| 73962 | (73204) | **GB** | GB | GBNR | SE | Dick Mabbutt |
| 73963 | (73206) | **GB** | GB | GBNR | SE | Janice |
| 73964 | (73205) | **GB** | GB | GBNR | SE | Jeanette |
| 73965 | (73208) | **GB** | GB | GBNR | SE | |

73966–971 are being rebuilt for work on the Caledonian Sleeper in Scotland and have no third rail electric capability. They also have a higher Train Supply index and a slightly higher fuel capacity.
**Fuel Capacity:** 1509 litres.          **Train Supply:** Electric, index 96.

73005 and 73006 were originally built at Eastleigh Works.

| | | | | | |
|---|---|---|---|---|---|
| 73966 | (73005) | **CA** | GB | GBCS | EC |
| 73967 | (73006) | **CA** | GB | GBCS | LB (S) |
| 73968 | (73117) | **CA** | GB | GBCS | LB (S) |
| 73969 | (73105) | | GB | GBCS | LB (S) |
| 73970 | (73103) | | GB | GBCS | LB (S) |
| 73971 | (73207) | | GB | GBCS | LB (S) |

---

# CLASS 86          BR/ENGLISH ELECTRIC          Bo-Bo

**Built:** 1965–66 by English Electric Co at Vulcan Foundry, Newton-le-Willows or by BR at Doncaster Works.
**Electric Supply System:** 25 kV AC 50 Hz overhead.
**Train Brakes:** Air.          **Brake Force:** 40 t.
**Dimensions:** 17.83 x 2.65 m.          **Weight:** 83–86.8 t.
**RA:** 6.          **Train Supply:** Electric, index 66.

Formerly numbered E3101–E3200 (not in order).

Class 86s exported for use abroad are listed in section 6 of this book.

**Class 86/1. Class 87-type bogies & motors.**

Details as above except:
**Traction Motors:** GEC 412AZ frame mounted.
**Maximum Tractive Effort:** 258 kN (58000 lbf).
**Continuous Rating:** 3730 kW (5000 hp) giving a tractive effort of 95 kN (21300 lbf) at 87 mph.
**Maximum Rail Power:** 5860 kW (7860 hp) at 50.8 mph.
**Wheel Diameter:** 1150 mm.          **Weight:** 86.8 t.
**Design Speed:** 110 mph.          **Maximum Speed:** 110 mph.

| | | | | | |
|---|---|---|---|---|---|
| 86101 | **CA** | EL | GBCH | WN | Sir William A Stanier FRS |

**Class 86/2. Standard design rebuilt with resilient wheels & Flexicoil suspension.**

**Traction Motors:** AEI 282BZ axle hung.
**Maximum Tractive Effort:** 207 kN (46500 lbf).

**Continuous Rating:** 3010 kW (4040 hp) giving a tractive effort of 85 kN (19200 lbf) at 77.5 mph.
**Maximum Rail Power:** 4550 kW (6100 hp) at 49.5 mph.
**Wheel Diameter:** 1156 mm.                    **Weight:** 85–86.2 t.
**Design Speed:** 125 mph.                      **Maximum Speed:** 100 mph.

**Non-standard livery:** 86259 BR "Electric blue". Also carries number E3137.

| 86229 | V | EP | EPEX | LM (S) | |
| 86231 | V | EP | EPEX | LM (S) | |
| 86234 | AR | EP | EPEX | LM (S) | |
| 86235 | AR | EP | EPUK | LR (S) | |
| 86246 | AR | EP | EPEX | WN (S) | |
| 86247 | EX | P | DHLT | BA (S) | |
| 86251 | V | EP | EPEX | LM (S) | |
| 86259 x | O | PP | MBEL | WN | Les Ross |

**Class 86/4.**

**Traction Motors:** AEI 282AZ axle hung.
**Maximum Tractive Effort:** 258 kN (58000 lbf).
**Continuous Rating:** 2680 kW (3600 hp) giving a tractive effort of 89 kN (20000 lbf) at 67 mph.
**Maximum Rail Power:** 4400 kW (5900 hp) at 38 mph.
**Wheel Diameter:** 1156 mm.                    **Weight:** 83–83.9 t.
**Design Speed:** 100 mph.                      **Maximum Speed:** 100 mph.

| 86401 | CA | EL | GBCH | WN | Mons Meg |

**Class 86/5. Regeared locomotive operated by Freightliner.**

Details as Class 86/4 except:

**Continuous Rating:** 2680 kW (3600 hp) giving a tractive effort of 117 kN (26300 lbf) at 67 mph.
**Maximum Speed:** 75 mph.                      **Train Supply:** Electric, isolated.

| 86501 (86608) | FL | FL | DFMC | CP |

**Class 86/6. Freightliner-operated locomotives.**

Details as Class 86/4 except:

**Maximum Speed:** 75 mph.                      **Train Supply:** Electric, isolated.

| 86604 | FL | FL | DFNC | CP |
| 86605 | FL | FL | DFNC | CP |
| 86607 | FL | FL | DFNC | CP |
| 86609 | FL | FL | DFNC | CP |
| 86610 | FL | FL | DFNC | CP |
| 86612 | FL | P | DFNC | CP |
| 86613 | FL | P | DFNC | CP |
| 86614 | FL | P | DFNC | CP |
| 86622 | FH | P | DFNC | CP |
| 86627 | FL | P | DFNC | CP |
| 86628 | FL | P | DFNC | CP |
| 86632 | FL | P | DFNC | CP |
| 86637 | FH | P | DFNC | CP |

| 86638 | **FL** | P | DFNC | CP |
| 86639 | **FL** | P | DFNC | CP |

**Class 86/7. Europhoenix-owned locomotives.** Refurbished Class 86/2s for the UK spot-hire market. Details as Class 86/2 unless stated.

**Maximum Speed:** 110 mph.　　　**Weight:** 85t.
**Train Supply:** Electric, index 74.

| 86701 | (86205) | **CS** | EP | EPUK | ZI (S) | Orion |
| 86702 | (86260) | **EL** | EP | EPUK | CR (S) | Cassiopeia |

# CLASS 87　　　　BREL/GEC　　　　Bo-Bo

**Built:** 1973–75 by BREL at Crewe Works.
**Electric Supply System:** 25 kV AC 50 Hz overhead.
**Traction Motors:** GEC G412AZ frame mounted.
**Maximum Tractive Effort:** 258 kN (58000 lbf).
**Continuous Rating:** 3730 kW (5000 hp) giving a tractive effort of 95 kN (21300 lbf) at 87 mph.
**Maximum Rail Power:** 5860 kW (7860 hp) at 50.8 mph.
**Train Brakes:** Air.　　　　　　**Brake Force:** 40 t.
**Dimensions:** 17.83 x 2.65 m.　　**Weight:** 83.3 t.
**Wheel Diameter:** 1150 mm.　　　**Design Speed:** 110 mph.
**Maximum Speed:** 110 mph.　　　**Train Supply:** Electric, index 95.
**RA:** 6.

Class 87s exported for use abroad are listed in section 6 of this book.

| 87002 | **CA** | EL | GBCH | WN | Royal Sovereign |

# CLASS 88　　　　VOSSLOH　　　　Bo-Bo

Ten new Vossloh bi-mode locomotives on order for DRS and due for delivery 2015–16. Full details awaited.
**Built:** 2015–16 by Vossloh, Valencia, Spain.
**Electric Supply System:** 25 kV AC 50 Hz overhead.
**Engine:** Caterpillar 12-cylinder 700 kW (940 hp) at 1800 rpm.
**Traction Motors:** ABB.
**Maximum Tractive Effort (Electric):**
**Maximum Tractive Effort (Diesel):**
**Continuous Rating:** 4000 kW (5360 hp).
**Maximum Rail Power:**　　　　　**Dimensions:**
**Train Brakes:** Air.　　　　　　**Brake Force:**
**Weight:**　　　　　　　　　　　**Wheel Diameter:**
**Fuel capacity:**　　　　　　　　**Train Supply:**
**Design Speed:** 100 mph.　　　　**Maximum Speed:** 100 mph.
**RA:**

| 88001 | BN |
| 88002 | BN |
| 88003 | BN |
| 88004 | BN |
| 88005 | BN |
| 88006 | BN |
| 88007 | BN |
| 88008 | BN |
| 88009 | BN |
| 88010 | BN |

## CLASS 90          GEC                          Bo-Bo

**Built:** 1987–90 by BREL at Crewe Works (as sub-contractors for GEC).
**Electric Supply System:** 25 kV AC 50 Hz overhead.
**Traction Motors:** GEC G412CY frame mounted.
**Maximum Tractive Effort:** 258 kN (58000 lbf).
**Continuous Rating:** 3730 kW (5000 hp) giving a tractive effort of 95 kN
(21300 lbf) at 87 mph.
**Maximum Rail Power:** 5860 kW (7860 hp) at 68.3 mph.
**Train Brakes:** Air.

| | |
|---|---|
| **Brake Force:** 40 t. | **Dimensions:** 18.80 x 2.74 m. |
| **Weight:** 84.5 t. | **Wheel Diameter:** 1150 mm. |
| **Design Speed:** 110 mph. | **Maximum Speed:** 110 mph. |
| **Train Supply:** Electric, index 95. | **RA:** 7. |

| 90001 b | GA | P | IANA | NC | Crown Point |
|---|---|---|---|---|---|
| 90002 b | GA | P | IANA | NC | Eastern Daily Press 1870–2010 SERVING NORFOLK FOR 140 YEARS |
| 90003 b | NX | P | IANA | NC | Rædwald of East Anglia |
| 90004 b | GA | P | IANA | NC | City of Chelmsford |
| 90005 b | GA | P | IANA | NC | Vice-Admiral Lord Nelson |
| 90006 b | 1 | P | IANA | NC | Modern Railways Magazine/ Roger Ford |
| 90007 b | 1 | P | IANA | NC | Sir John Betjeman |
| 90008 b | NX | P | IANA | NC | The East Anglian |
| 90009 b | 1 | P | IANA | NC | Diamond Jubilee |
| 90010 b | GA | P | IANA | NC | |
| 90011 b | GA | P | IANA | NC | East Anglian Daily Times Suffolk & Proud |
| 90012 b | GA | P | IANA | NC | Royal Anglian Regiment |
| 90013 b | GA | P | IANA | NC | |
| 90014 b | GA | P | IANA | NC | Norfolk and Norwich Festival |
| 90015 b | GA | P | IANA | NC | Colchester Castle |
| 90016 | FL | P | DFLC | CP | |
| 90017 | E | DB | WQBA | CE (S) | |
| 90018 | DB | DB | WEAC | CE | |
| 90019 | FS | DB | WQAA | CE (S) | |
| 90020 | E | DB | WEAC | CE | Collingwood |
| 90021 | FS | DB | WEAC | CE | |
| 90022 | EG | DB | WQBA | CE (S) | Freightconnection |
| 90023 | E | DB | WQBA | CE (S) | |

| 90024 | FS | DB | WEAC | CE |  |
|-------|-----|-----|------|-------|---|
| 90025 | F  | DB | WQBA | CE (S) |  |
| 90026 | E  | DB | WQAA | CE (S) |  |
| 90027 | F  | DB | WQBA | CE (S) | Allerton T&RS Depot |
| 90028 | E  | DB | WEAC | CE |  |
| 90029 | DB | DB | WEAC | CE |  |
| 90030 | E  | DB | WQBA | CE (S) |  |
| 90031 | E  | DB | WQBA | CE (S) | The Railway Children Partnership |
|       |    |    |      |        | Working For Street Children Worldwide |
| 90032 | E  | DB | WQBA | CE (S) |  |
| 90033 | FE | DB | WQBA | CE (S) |  |
| 90034 | DR | DB | WEAC | CE |  |
| 90035 | E  | DB | WEAC | CE |  |
| 90036 | DB | DB | WEDC | CE | Driver Jack Mills |
| 90037 | E  | DB | WEDC | CE | Spirit of Dagenham |
| 90038 | FE | DB | WQBA | CE (S) |  |
| 90039 | E  | DB | WEAC | CE |  |
| 90040 | E  | DB | WQAA | CE (S) | The Railway Mission |
| 90041 | FL | P  | DFLC | CP |  |
| 90042 | FH | P  | DFLC | CP |  |
| 90043 | FF | P  | DFLC | CP |  |
| 90044 | FF | P  | DFLC | CP |  |
| 90045 | FH | P  | DFLC | CP |  |
| 90046 | FL | P  | DFLC | CP |  |
| 90047 | FF | P  | DFLC | CP |  |
| 90048 | FF | P  | DFLC | CP |  |
| 90049 | FH | P  | DFLC | CP |  |
| 90050 | FF | AV | DHLT | BA (S) |  |

# CLASS 91          GEC                          Bo-Bo

**Built:** 1988–91 by BREL at Crewe Works (as sub-contractors for GEC).
**Electric Supply System:** 25 kV AC 50 Hz overhead.
**Traction Motors:** GEC G426AZ.
**Maximum Tractive Effort:** 190 kN (43 000 lbf).
**Continuous Rating:** 4540 kW (6090 hp) giving a tractive effort of 170 kN at 96 mph.
**Maximum Rail Power:** 4700 kW (6300 hp) at ?? mph.
**Train Brakes:** Air.
**Brake Force:** 45 t.
**Weight:** 84 t.
**Design Speed:** 140 mph.
**Train Supply:** Electric, index 95.

**Dimensions:** 19.41 x 2.74 m.
**Wheel Diameter:** 1000 mm.
**Maximum Speed:** 125 mph.
**RA:** 7.

Locomotives were originally numbered in the 910xx series, but were renumbered upon completion of overhauls at Bombardier, Doncaster by the addition of 100 to their original number. The exception to this rule was 91023 which was renumbered 91132.

91114 has been fitted with a second pantograph for evaluation purposes.

**Advertising liveries:**

91101 Flying Scotsman (purple).

91110 Battle of Britain (black and grey).

91111 For the fallen (various with poppy and Union Jack vinyls).

| 91101 | **AL** | E | IECA | BN | |
|-------|--------|---|------|----|---|
| 91102 | **EC** | E | IECA | BN | City of York |
| 91103 | **VE** | E | IECA | BN | |
| 91104 | **EC** | E | IECA | BN | |
| 91105 | **VE** | E | IECA | BN | |
| 91106 | **EC** | E | IECA | BN | |
| 91107 | **VE** | E | IECA | BN | SKYFALL |
| 91108 | **VE** | E | IECA | BN | |
| 91109 | **EC** | E | IECA | BN | Sir Bobby Robson |
| 91110 | **AL** | E | IECA | BN | BATTLE OF BRITAIN MEMORIAL FLIGHT |
| 91111 | **AL** | E | IECA | BN | For the Fallen |
| 91112 | **VE** | E | IECA | BN | |
| 91113 | **VE** | E | IECA | BN | |
| 91114 | **VE** | E | IECA | BN | Durham Cathedral |
| 91115 | **VE** | E | IECA | BN | Blaydon Races |
| 91116 | **VE** | E | IECA | BN | |
| 91117 | **EC** | E | IECA | BN | WEST RIDING LIMITED |
| 91118 | **EC** | E | IECA | BN | |
| 91119 | **EC** | E | IECA | BN | |
| 91120 | **EC** | E | IECA | BN | |
| 91121 | **VE** | E | IECA | BN | |
| 91122 | **VE** | E | IECA | BN | |
| 91124 | **VE** | E | IECA | BN | |
| 91125 | **EC** | E | IECA | BN | |
| 91126 | **VE** | E | IECA | BN | |
| 91127 | **EC** | E | IECA | BN | |
| 91128 | **EC** | E | IECA | BN | |
| 91129 | **VE** | E | IECA | BN | |
| 91130 | **EC** | E | IECA | BN | |
| 91131 | **VE** | E | IECA | BN | |
| 91132 | **VE** | E | IECA | BN | |

---

# CLASS 92          BRUSH                    Co-Co

**Built:** 1993–96 by Brush Traction at Loughborough.
**Electric Supply System:** 25 kV AC 50 Hz overhead or 750 V DC third rail.
**Traction Motors:** Asea Brown Boveri design. Model 6FRA 7059B (Asynchronous 3-phase induction motors).
**Maximum Tractive Effort:** 400 kN (90 000 lbf).
**Continuous Rating:** 5040 kW (6760 hp) on AC, 4000 kW (5360 hp) on DC.

| | |
|---|---|
| **Maximum Rail Power:** | **Train Brakes:** Air. |
| **Brake Force:** 63 t. | **Dimensions:** 21.34 x 2.67 m. |
| **Weight:** 126 t. | **Wheel Diameter:** 1070 mm. |

**Design Speed:** 140 km/h (87 mph). **Maximum Speed:** 145 km/h (90 mph).
**Train Supply:** Electric, index 108 (AC), 70 (DC).
**RA:** 7.

\* Modified to operate on High Speed 1.

Class 92s exported for use abroad are listed in section 6 of this book.

**Advertising livery:** 92017 Stobart Rail (two-tone blue & white).

| | | | | | | |
|---|---|---|---|---|---|---|
| 92003 | * | **EG** | DB | WGEE | CE (S) | Beethoven |
| 92004 | | **EG** | DB | WQBA | CE (S) | Jane Austen |
| 92006 | | **EP** | GB | GBET | LB (S) | Louis Armand |
| 92007 | | **EG** | DB | WQBA | CE (S) | Schubert |
| 92008 | | **EG** | DB | WQBA | CE (S) | Jules Verne |
| 92009 | * | **DB** | DB | WQBA | CE (S) | Marco Polo |
| 92010 | | **CA** | GB | GBST | WN | |
| 92011 | | **EG** | DB | WFBC | CE | Handel |
| 92013 | | **EG** | DB | WQAA | CE (S) | Puccini |
| 92014 | | **CA** | GB | GBSL | WN | |
| 92015 | * | **DB** | DB | WFBC | CE | |
| 92016 | * | **DB** | DB | WFBC | CE | |
| 92017 | | **AL** | DB | WQBA | CE (S) | Bart the Engine |
| 92018 | | **CA** | GB | GBSL | WN | |
| 92019 | | **EG** | DB | WFBC | CE | Wagner |
| 92020 | | **EP** | GB | GBET | LB (S) | Milton |
| 92021 | | **EP** | GB | GBET | CO (S) | Purcell |
| 92022 | | **EG** | DB | WQBA | CE (S) | Charles Dickens |
| 92023 | | **CA** | GB | GBST | WN | |
| 92026 | | **EG** | DB | WQBA | CE (S) | Britten |
| 92028 | | **GB** | GB | GBST | WN | |
| 92029 | | **EG** | DB | WGEE | CE (S) | Dante |
| 92031 | * | **DB** | DB | WQAA | CE (S) | |
| 92032 | | **GB** | GB | GBST | WN | IMechE Railway Division |
| 92033 | | **CA** | GB | GBSL | WN | |
| 92035 | | **EP** | DB | WQBA | CE (S) | Mendelssohn |
| 92036 | * | **EG** | DB | WFBC | CE | Bertolt Brecht |
| 92037 | | **EG** | DB | WQAA | CE (S) | Sullivan |
| 92038 | | **CA** | GB | GBST | WN | |
| 92040 | | **EP** | GB | GBET | CO (S) | Goethe |
| 92041 | * | **EG** | DB | WQAA | CE (S) | Vaughan Williams |
| 92042 | * | **DB** | DB | WFBC | CE | |
| 92043 | | **EP** | GB | GBST | WN | Debussy |
| 92044 | | **EP** | GB | GBST | WN | Couperin |
| 92045 | | **EP** | GB | GBET | LB (S) | Chaucer |
| 92046 | | **EP** | GB | GBET | LB (S) | Sweelinck |

# 3. EUROTUNNEL LOCOMOTIVES

## DIESEL LOCOMOTIVES

### 0001–0007        MaK                        Bo-Bo

**Built:** 1991–92 by MaK at Kiel, Germany (Model DE1004).
**Engine:** MTU 12V 396 TC13 of 940 kW (1260 hp) at 1800 rpm.
**Main Alternator:** ABB.            **Traction Motors:** ABB.
**Maximum Tractive Effort:** 305 kN (68600 lbf).
**Continuous Tractive Effort:** 140 kN (31500 lbf) at 20 mph.
**Power At Rail:** 750 kW (1012 hp).   **Dimensions:** 14.40 x ?? m.
**Brake Force:** 120 kN.             **Wheel Diameter:** 1000 mm.
**Weight:** 82 t.                    **Maximum Speed:** 100 km/h.
**Design Speed:** 120 km/h.          **Train Brakes:** Air.
**Fuel Capacity:** 3500 litres.      **Multiple Working:** Within class.
**Train Supply:** Not equipped.      **Signalling System:** TVM430 cab signalling.

Registered on TOPS as 21901–907.

| | | | |
|---|---|---|---|
| 0001 | **GY** | ET | CO |
| 0002 | **GY** | ET | CO |
| 0003 | **GY** | ET | CO |
| 0004 | **GY** | ET | CO |
| 0005 | **GY** | ET | CO |

The following two locos were rebuilt from NS 6400 Class 6456 and 6457 (built 1991) and added to the Eurotunnel fleet in 2011.

| | | | |
|---|---|---|---|
| 0006 | **GY** | ET | CO |
| 0007 | **GY** | ET | CO |

### 0031–0042        HUNSLET/SCHÖMA              0-4-0

**Built:** 1989–90 by Hunslet Engine Company at Leeds as 900 mm gauge.
**Rebuilt:** 1993–94 by Schöma in Germany to 1435 mm gauge.
**Engine:** Deutz FL10L 413FW of 170 kW (230 hp) at 2300 rpm.
**Transmission:** Mechanical Clark 5000 series.
**Maximum Tractive Effort:**
**Continuous Tractive Effort:**
**Power At Rail:**
**Brake Force:**                     **Dimensions:** 6.63 x 2.69 m.
**Weight:** 26–28 t.                 **Wheel Diameter:**
**Design Speed:** 48 km/h.           **Maximum Speed:** 50 km/h.
**Fuel Capacity:**                   **Train Brakes:** Air.
**Train Supply:** Not equipped.      **Multiple Working:** Not equipped.

* Rebuilt with inspection platforms to check overhead catenary.

▲ DBS-liveried 60059 passes Branston, near Burton-upon-Trent, with 6M57 07.15 Lindsey–Kingsbury loaded bogie tanks. **Paul Biggs**

▼ Colas Rail-liveried 66848 is on hire to Freightliner as it works 4O29 08.14 Crewe–Southampton through Tilehurst on 09/08/14. **Mark Few**

▲ DBS-liveried 67027 passes Loughborough with a London St Pancras–Derby test train on 12/06/14 (67029 was on the rear). **Paul Biggs**

▼ Freightliner-liveried 70020 and 70018 double head 4O55 12.12 Leeds–Southampton intermodal at Dunston, south of Lincoln, on 06/02/15. **Nick Edmonds**

▲ ScotRail Saltire-liveried 68007 is seen near Greenhill Lower Junction with the 18.24 Cardenden–Mossend empty stock on 05/06/15. **Robin Ralston**

▲ Freightliner PowerHaul-liveried 86622 leads Freightliner grey-liveried 90043 (one of the few pre-privatisation liveries still around) at Lamington with 4M11 18.23 Coatbridge–Crewe on 19/06/13.
**Robin Ralston**

▲ GBRf-liveried 73961, 73965 and 73964 stabled in Tonbridge West Yard on 15/08/15. **Stuart Hicks**

▼ Caledonian Sleeper-liveried 86101 passes Hemel Hempstead on 21/04/15, leading 92028 on a Bletchley–Willesden test run. **Alisdair Anderson**

▲ Caledonian Sleeper-liveried 87002 hauls the southbound Inverness–London Euston Highland Sleeper at Old Linslade on 21/04/15.    **Alisdair Anderson**

▼ DB Schenker-liveried 90029 is seen stabled in Wembley Yard on 17/10/14.
**Brian Denton**

▲ Virgin Trains East Coast-liveried 91108 hauls a London King's Cross–Leeds service north near Biggleswade on 21/04/15.　　**Alisdair Anderson**

▼ MaK Eurotunnel rescue locomotives 0003, 0007 (ex-NS) and 0002 haul new Eurostar 4017/18 from Calais Fréthun to Temple Mills depot near Sevington on 04/03/15.　　**Tony Christie**

▲ Caledonian Sleeper-liveried 92018 passes Old Linslade with the southbound Inverness–London Euston Highland Sleeper on 18/07/15. **Andrew Mason**

| 0031 |   | **GY** | ET | CO | FRANCES |
|------|---|--------|----|----|---------|
| 0032 |   | **GY** | ET | CO | ELISABETH |
| 0033 |   | **GY** | ET | CO | SILKE |
| 0034 |   | **GY** | ET | CO | AMANDA |
| 0035 |   | **GY** | ET | CO | MARY |
| 0036 |   | **GY** | ET | CO | LAURENCE |
| 0037 |   | **GY** | ET | CO | LYDIE |
| 0038 |   | **GY** | ET | CO | JENNY |
| 0039 | * | **GY** | ET | CO | PACITA |
| 0040 |   | **GY** | ET | CO | JILL |
| 0041 | * | **GY** | ET | CO | KIM |
| 0042 |   | **GY** | ET | CO | NICOLE |

## ELECTRIC LOCOMOTIVES

## 9005–9840          BRUSH/ABB          Bo-Bo-Bo

**Built:** 1993–2002 by Brush Traction at Loughborough.
**Supply System:** 25 kV AC 50 Hz overhead.
**Traction Motors:** Asea Brown Boveri design. Asynchronous 3-phase motors.
Model 6FHA 7059 (as built). Model 6FHA 7059C (7000 kW rated locos).
**Maximum Tractive Effort:** 400kN (90 000 lbf).
**Continuous Rating:** Class 9/0 and 9/1: 5760 kW (7725 hp). Class 9/7 and 9/8:
7000 kW (9387 hp).

| **Maximum Rail Power:** | **Multiple Working:** TDM system. |
|---|---|
| **Brake Force:** 50 t. | **Dimensions:** 22.01 x 2.97 x 4.20 m. |
| **Weight:** 136 t. | **Wheel Diameter:** 1250 mm. |
| **Design Speed:** 100 mph. | **Maximum Speed:** 100 mph. |
| **Train Supply:** Electric. | **Train Brakes:** Air. |

**Class 9/0 Original build locos.** Built 1993–94.

| 9005 | **EB** | ET | CO | JESSYE NORMAN |
|------|--------|----|----|---------------|
| 9007 | **EB** | ET | CO | DAME JOAN SUTHERLAND |
| 9011 | **EB** | ET | CO | JOSÉ VAN DAM |
| 9013 | **EB** | ET | CO | MARIA CALLAS |
| 9015 | **EB** | ET | CO | LÖTSCHBERG 1913 |
| 9018 | **EB** | ET | CO | WILHELMENIA FERNANDEZ |
| 9022 | **EB** | ET | CO | DAME JANET BAKER |
| 9024 | **EB** | ET | CO | GOTTHARD 1882 |
| 9026 | **EB** | ET | CO | FURKATUNNEL 1982 |
| 9029 | **EB** | ET | CO | THOMAS ALLEN |
| 9033 | **EB** | ET | CO | MONTSERRAT CABALLE |
| 9036 | **EB** | ET | CO | ALAIN FONDARY |
| 9037 | **EB** | ET | CO | GABRIEL BACQUIER |

**Class 9/7. Increased power freight shuttle locos.** Built 2001–02 (9711–23
built 1998–2001 as 9101–13 and rebuilt as 9711–23 2010–12).

| 9701 | **EB** | ET | CO |
|------|--------|----|----|
| 9702 | **EB** | ET | CO |

| 9703 | **EB** | ET | CO |
| 9704 | **EB** | ET | CO |
| 9705 | **EB** | ET | CO |
| 9706 | **EB** | ET | CO |
| 9707 | **EB** | ET | CO |

| 9711 | (9101) | **EB** | ET | CO |
| 9712 | (9102) | **EB** | ET | CO |
| 9713 | (9103) | **EB** | ET | CO |
| 9714 | (9104) | **EB** | ET | CO |
| 9715 | (9105) | **EB** | ET | CO |
| 9716 | (9106) | **EB** | ET | CO |
| 9717 | (9107) | **EB** | ET | CO |
| 9718 | (9108) | **EB** | ET | CO |
| 9719 | (9109) | **EB** | ET | CO |
| 9720 | (9110) | **EB** | ET | CO |
| 9721 | (9111) | **EB** | ET | CO |
| 9722 | (9112) | **EB** | ET | CO |
| 9723 | (9113) | **EB** | ET | CO |

**Class 9/8 Locos rebuilt from Class 9/0 by adding 800 to the loco number. Uprated to 7000 kW.**

| 9801 | **EB** | ET | CO |     | LESLEY GARRETT |
| 9802 | **EB** | ET | CO |     | STUART BURROWS |
| 9803 | **EB** | ET | CO |     | BENJAMIN LUXON |
| 9804 | **EB** | ET | CO |     | VICTORIA DE LOS ANGELES |
| 9806 | **EB** | ET | CO |     | REGINE CRESPIN |
| 9808 | **EB** | ET | CO |     | ELISABETH SODERSTROM |
| 9809 | **EB** | ET | CO |     | FRANÇOISE POLLET |
| 9810 | **EB** | ET | CO |     | JEAN-PHILIPPE COURTIS |
| 9812 | **EB** | ET | CO |     | LUCIANO PAVAROTTI |
| 9814 | **EB** | ET | CO |     | LUCIA POPP |
| 9816 | **EB** | ET | CO |     | WILLARD WHITE |
| 9817 | **EB** | ET | CO | (S) | JOSÉ CARRERAS |
| 9819 | **EB** | ET | CO |     | MARIA EWING |
| 9820 | **EB** | ET | CO |     | NICOLAI GHIAROV |
| 9821 | **EB** | ET | CO |     | TERESA BERGANZA |
| 9823 | **EB** | ET | CO |     | DAME ELISABETH LEGGE-SCHWARZKOPF |
| 9825 | **EB** | ET | CO |     | |
| 9827 | **EB** | ET | CO |     | BARBARA HENDRICKS |
| 9828 | **EB** | ET | CO |     | DAME KIRI TE KANAWA |
| 9831 | **EB** | ET | CO |     | |
| 9832 | **EB** | ET | CO |     | RENATA TEBALDI |
| 9834 | **EB** | ET | CO |     | MIRELLA FRENI |
| 9835 | **EB** | ET | CO |     | NICOLAI GEDDA |
| 9838 | **EB** | ET | CO |     | HILDEGARD BEHRENS |
| 9840 | **EB** | ET | CO |     | |

# 4. FORMER BR MAIN LINE LOCOS IN INDUSTRIAL SERVICE

Former British Rail main line locomotives considered to be in "industrial use" are listed here. These locomotives do not currently have Network Rail engineering acceptance for operation on the national railway network.

*Number  Other no./name     Location*

**Class 03**

| | | |
|---|---|---|
| 03084 | HELEN-LOUISE | West Coast Railway Company, Carnforth |
| 03179 | CLIVE | Govia Thameslink Railway, Hornsey Depot, London |
| 03196 | JOYCE/GLYNIS | West Coast Railway Company, Carnforth |
| D2381 | | West Coast Railway Company, Carnforth |

**Class 07**

| | | |
|---|---|---|
| D2991 | 07007 | Arlington Fleet Services, Eastleigh Works, Hampshire |

**Class 08**

| | | |
|---|---|---|
| 08220 | | EMD, Longport Works, Stoke-on-Trent |
| | | *(on loan from Nottingham Transport Heritage Centre)* |
| 08308 | 23 | PD Ports, Teesport, Grangetown, Middlesbrough |
| 08331 | | Midland Railway-Butterley, Derbyshire |
| 08375 | 21 | Hanson Cement, Ketton Cement Works, nr Stamford |
| 08389 | | Barrow Hill Roundhouse, Chesterfield, Derbyshire |
| 08393 | | LH Group, Barton-under-Needwood, Staffordshire |
| 08401 | | LH Group, Barton-under-Needwood, Staffordshire |
| 08411 | | RSS, Rye Farm, Wishaw, Sutton Coldfield |
| 08418 | | West Coast Railway Company, Carnforth |
| 08423 | H011  14 | PD Ports, Teesport, Grangetown, Middlesbrough |
| 08441 | | RSS, Rye Farm, Wishaw, Sutton Coldfield |
| 08442 | | Arriva TrainCare, Eastleigh Depot, Hampshire |
| 08445 | | Daventry International Railfreight Terminal, Crick |
| 08447 | | John G Russell (Transport), Hillington, Glasgow |
| 08460 | | RSS, Rye Farm, Wishaw, Sutton Coldfield |
| 08484 | CAPTAIN NATHANIEL DARELL | National Railway Museum, Shildon, County Durham |
| 08485 | | West Coast Railway Company, Carnforth |
| 08499 | | Colas Rail, Canton Depot, Cardiff |
| 08500 | | Tees Yard *(awaiting collection)* |
| 08502 | | Barrow Hill Roundhouse, Chesterfield, Derbyshire |
| 08503 | | Barry Island Railway, Vale of Glamorgan |
| 08507 | | LNWR Heritage Company, Crewe, Cheshire |
| 08511 | | Felixstowe Dock & Railway Company, Felixstowe |
| 08516 | | Arriva TrainCare, Barton Hill Depot, Bristol |
| 08527 | | Northern, Allerton Depot, Liverpool |
| 08536 | | RVEL, RTC Business Park, Derby |
| 08568 | St. Rollox | Knorr-Bremse Rail Systems, Springburn Depot, Glasgow |
| 08573 | | Bombardier Transportation, Ilford Works, London |
| 08588 | | Cemex UK, Washwood Heath, Birmingham |
| 08598 | H016 HERCULES | Chasewater Light Railway, Brownhills, Staffordshire |

| 08600 | | AV Dawson, Ayrton Rail Terminal, Middlesbrough |
|---|---|---|
| 08602 | 004 BOMBER | Bombardier Transportation, Derby Works |
| 08613 | H064 | Celtic Energy, Onllwyn Coal & Distribution Centre, W Glamorgan |
| 08622 | H028 19 | Hanson Cement, Ketton Cement Works, nr Stamford |
| 08629 | Wolverton | Knorr-Bremse Rail Systems, Wolverton Works, Milton Keynes |
| 08631 | | LNWR Heritage Company, Crewe, Cheshire |
| 08643 | | Aggregate Industries, Merehead Rail Terminal |
| 08648 | | Northern, Heaton Depot, Newcastle-upon-Tyne |
| 08649 | Bradwell | Knorr-Bremse Rail Systems, Wolverton Works, Milton Keynes |
| 08650 | ISLE OF GRAIN | Bardon Aggregates, Isle of Grain, Kent |
| 08652 | | Hanson Aggregates, Whatley Quarry, near Frome |
| 08670 | | RSS, Rye Farm, Wishaw, Sutton Coldfield |
| 08678 | ARTILA | West Coast Railway Company, Carnforth |
| 08682 | Lionheart | Bombardier Transportation, Derby Works |
| 08683 | | Bombardier Transportation, Derby Works |
| 08685 | | Barrow Hill Roundhouse, Chesterfield, Derbyshire |
| 08699 | | Weardale Railway, Wolsingham, County Durham |
| 08700 | | Bombardier Transportation, Ilford Works, London |
| 08704 | | LNWR Heritage Company, Crewe, Cheshire |
| 08711 | | Tees Yard *(awaiting collection)* |
| 08730 | The Caley | Knorr-Bremse Rail Systems, Springburn Depot, Glasgow |
| 08738 | | Colne Valley Railway, Halstead, Essex |
| 08743 | Bryan Turner | SembCorp Utilities Teesside, Wilton, Middlesbrough |
| 08750 | | Weardale Railway, Wolsingham, County Durham |
| 08756 | | Tata Steel, Shotton Works, Deeside, Flintshire |
| 08762 | | Cemex UK, Washwood Heath, Birmingham |
| 08764 | | Stonebridge Park Heavy Repair depot, Wembley, London |
| 08765 | | Barrow Hill Roundhouse, Chesterfield, Derbyshire |
| 08774 | ARTHUR VERNON DAWSON | AV Dawson, Ayrton Rail Terminal, Middlesbrough |
| 08786 | | Barrow Hill Roundhouse, Chesterfield, Derbyshire |
| 08787 | "08296" | Hanson Aggregates, Machen Quarry, nr Newport |
| 08807 | | AV Dawson, Ayrton Rail Terminal, Middlesbrough |
| 08809 | 24 | PD Ports, Teesport, Grangetown, Middlesbrough |
| 08810 | RICHARD J. WENHAM EASTLEIGH DEPOT | Arriva TrainCare, Eastleigh Depot, Hampshire |
| 08818 | MOLLY | Celsa Steel UK, Tremorfa Steelworks, Cardiff |
| 08823 | LIBBIE | Daventry International Railfreight Terminal, Crick |
| 08834 | | Barrow Hill Roundhouse, Chesterfield, Derbyshire |
| 08846 | 003 | RSS, Rye Farm, Wishaw, Sutton Coldfield |
| 08868 | | Arriva TrainCare, Crewe Depot, Cheshire |
| 08870 | H024 | Weardale Railway, Wolsingham, County Durham |
| 08871 | 22 | Weardale Railway, Wolsingham, County Durham |
| 08873 | | Hams Hall Distribution Park, Coleshill, Warwickshire |
| 08877 | | Wigan Springs Branch Depot *(awaiting collection)* |
| 08885 | H042 18 | Weardale Railway, Wolsingham, County Durham |
| 08892 | | Bombardier Transportation, Old Dalby Test Centre, Asfordby |
| 08903 | JOHN W. ANTILL | SembCorp Utilities Teesside, Wilton, Middlesbrough |
| 08905 | | Hope Construction Materials, Hope Cement Works, Derbyshire |
| 08912 | | AV Dawson, Ayrton Rail Terminal, Middlesbrough |
| 08913 | | LH Group, Barton-under-Needwood, Staffordshire |

| | |
|---|---|
| 08918 | Nemesis Rail, Burton-upon-Trent, Staffordshire |
| 08924 1 | GB Railfreight, Garston Car Terminal, Liverpool |
| 08927 D4157 | EMD, Roberts Road Depot, Doncaster |
| 08933 | Aggregate Industries, Merehead Rail Terminal |
| 08936 | Tata Steel, Shotton Works, Deeside, Flintshire |
| 08937 D4167 | Bardon Aggregates, Meldon Quarry, near Okehampton |
| 08939 | RSS, Rye Farm, Wishaw, Sutton Coldfield |
| 08943 | Bombardier Transportation, Central Rivers Depot, Barton |
| 08947 HOWIE | Arlington Fleet Services, Eastleigh Works, Hampshire |
| 08956 | Bombardier Transportation, Old Dalby Test Centre, Asfordby |
| 08994 | Nemesis Rail, Burton-upon-Trent, Staffordshire |

### Class 09

| | |
|---|---|
| 09006 | Nemesis Rail, Burton-upon-Trent, Staffordshire |
| 09007 D3671 | London Overground, Willesden Depot, London |
| 09014 | Nemesis Rail, Burton-upon-Trent, Staffordshire |
| 09022 | Victoria Group, Port of Boston, Boston |
| 09201 | Hope Construction Materials, Hope Cement Works, Derbyshire |
| 09204 | Arriva TrainCare, Crewe Depot, Cheshire |

### Class 14

| | |
|---|---|
| D9504 | Kent & East Sussex Railway |
| D9529 14029 | Nene Valley Railway |

### Class 20

| | |
|---|---|
| 20056 81 | Tata Steel, Appleby-Frodingham Works, Scunthorpe |
| 20066 82 | Tata Steel, Appleby-Frodingham Works, Scunthorpe |
| 20110 D8110 | Tata Steel, Appleby-Frodingham Works, Scunthorpe |
| 20121 | Barrow Hill Roundhouse, Chesterfield, Derbyshire |
| 20166 | Wensleydale Railway, Leeming Bar, North Yorkshire |
| 20168 2 SIR GEORGE EARLE | Hope Construction Materials, Hope Cement Works, Derbyshire |
| 20906 3 | Hope Construction Materials, Hope Cement Works, Derbyshire |

### Class 47

| | |
|---|---|
| 47703 | Wabtec Rail, Doncaster Works |
| 47714 | Bombardier Transportation, Old Dalby Test Centre, Asfordby |

# 5. LOCOMOTIVES AWAITING DISPOSAL

Locomotives that are still extant but at scrapyards are listed here.

### Class 08

| | | | |
|---|---|---|---|
| 08646 | EMR, Kingsbury | 08872 | EMR, Attercliffe |
| 08783 | EMR, Kingsbury | 08921 | EMR, Kingsbury |
| 08798 | EMR, Attercliffe | | |

### Class 09

| | | | |
|---|---|---|---|
| 09023 | EMR, Attercliffe | 09107 | EMR, Kingsbury |

### Class 86

| | | | |
|---|---|---|---|
| 86901 | CF Booth, Rotherham | 86902 | CF Booth, Rotherham |

# 6. LOCOMOTIVES EXPORTED FOR USE ABROAD

This section details former BR (plus privatisation era) diesel and electric locomotives that have been exported from the UK for use in industrial locations or by a main line operator abroad. Not included are locos that are "preserved" abroad, which are included in our "Preserved Locomotives of British Railways" publication. (S) denotes locomotives that are stored.

*Number  Other no./name    Location*

**Class 03**

| | |
|---|---|
| D2xxx | Ferramento Pugliesse, Terlizzi, Bari, Italy |

**Class 04**

| | |
|---|---|
| D2289 | Lonato SpA, Lonato Steelworks, Lonato, Brescia, Italy |

**Class 47**

| | |
|---|---|
| 47375 | Continental Railway Solution, Hungary |

**Class 56**

| | | |
|---|---|---|
| 56101 | 0659 001-5 | FLOYD, Hungary |
| 56115 | 0659 002-3 | FLOYD, Hungary |
| 56117 | 0659 003-1 | FLOYD, Hungary (S) |

**Class 58**

| | | |
|---|---|---|
| 58001 | | Axiom Rail, France, (S) Alizay |
| 58004 | | Axiom Rail, France, (S) Alizay |
| 58005 | | Axiom Rail, France, (S) Alizay |
| 58006 | | Axiom Rail, France, (S) Alizay |
| 58007 | | Axiom Rail, France, (S) Alizay |
| 58009 | | Axiom Rail, France, (S) Alizay |
| 58010 | | Axiom Rail, France, (S) Alizay |
| 58011 | | Axiom Rail, France, (S) Alizay |
| 58013 | | Axiom Rail, France, (S) Alizay |
| 58015 | | Transfesa, Spain, (S) Monforte del Cid, Alicante |
| 58018 | | Axiom Rail, France, (S) Alizay |
| 58020 | L43 | Transfesa, Spain, (S) Monforte del Cid, Alicante |
| 58021 | | Axiom Rail, France, (S) Alizay |
| 58024 | L42 | Transfesa, Spain, (S) Monforte del Cid, Alicante |
| 58025 | | DB Schenker, Spain, (S) Albacete |
| 58026 | | Axiom Rail, France, (S) Alizay |
| 58027 | L52 | DB Schenker, Spain, (S) Albacete |
| 58029 | L44 | Transfesa, Spain, (S) Monforte del Cid, Alicante |
| 58030 | L46 | Transfesa, Spain, (S) Monforte del Cid, Alicante |
| 58031 | L45 | Transfesa, Spain, (S) Monforte del Cid, Alicante |
| 58032 | | Axiom Rail, France, (S) Alizay |
| 58033 | | Axiom Rail, France, (S) Alizay |
| 58034 | | Axiom Rail, France, (S) Alizay |

| | | |
|---|---|---|
| 58035 | | Axiom Rail, France, (S) Alizay |
| 58036 | | Axiom Rail, France, (S) Alizay |
| 58038 | | Axiom Rail, France, (S) Alizay |
| 58039 | | Axiom Rail, France, (S) Alizay |
| 58040 | | Axiom Rail, France, (S) Alizay |
| 58041 | L36 | Transfesa, Spain, (S) Albacete |
| 58042 | | Axiom Rail, France, (S) Alizay |
| 58043 | L37 | Transfesa, Spain, (S) Monforte del Cid, Alicante |
| 58044 | | Axiom Rail, France, (S) Woippy, Metz |
| 58046 | | Axiom Rail, France, (S) Alizay |
| 58047 | L51 | Transfesa, Spain, (S) Monforte del Cid, Alicante |
| 58049 | | Axiom Rail, France, (S) Alizay |
| 58050 | L53 | DB Schenker, Spain, (S) Albacete |

**Class 66**

| | |
|---|---|
| 66010 | Euro Cargo Rail, France |
| 66022 | Euro Cargo Rail, France |
| 66026 | Euro Cargo Rail, France |
| 66028 | Euro Cargo Rail, France |
| 66029 | Euro Cargo Rail, France |
| 66032 | Euro Cargo Rail, France |
| 66033 | Euro Cargo Rail, France |
| 66036 | Euro Cargo Rail, France |
| 66038 | Euro Cargo Rail, France |
| 66042 | Euro Cargo Rail, France |
| 66045 | Euro Cargo Rail, France |
| 66049 | Euro Cargo Rail, France |
| 66052 | Euro Cargo Rail, France |
| 66062 | Euro Cargo Rail, France |
| 66064 | Euro Cargo Rail, France |
| 66071 | Euro Cargo Rail, France |
| 66072 | Euro Cargo Rail, France |
| 66073 | Euro Cargo Rail, France |
| 66123 | Euro Cargo Rail, France |
| 66146 | DB Schenker Rail Polska, Poland |
| 66153 | DB Schenker Rail Polska, Poland |
| 66157 | DB Schenker Rail Polska, Poland |
| 66159 | DB Schenker Rail Polska, Poland |
| 66163 | DB Schenker Rail Polska, Poland |
| 66166 | DB Schenker Rail Polska, Poland |
| 66173 | DB Schenker Rail Polska, Poland |
| 66178 | DB Schenker Rail Polska, Poland |
| 66179 | Euro Cargo Rail, France |
| 66180 | DB Schenker Rail Polska, Poland |
| 66189 | DB Schenker Rail Polska, Poland |
| 66190 | Euro Cargo Rail, France |
| 66191 | Euro Cargo Rail, France |
| 66195 | Euro Cargo Rail, France |
| 66196 | DB Schenker Rail Polska, Poland |
| 66202 | Euro Cargo Rail, France |
| 66203 | Euro Cargo Rail, France |

| | | |
|---|---|---|
| 66205 | | Euro Cargo Rail, France |
| 66208 | | Euro Cargo Rail, France |
| 66209 | | Euro Cargo Rail, France |
| 66210 | | Euro Cargo Rail, France |
| 66211 | | Euro Cargo Rail, France |
| 66212 | | Euro Cargo Rail, France |
| 66214 | | Euro Cargo Rail, France |
| 66215 | | Euro Cargo Rail, France |
| 66216 | | Euro Cargo Rail, France |
| 66217 | | Euro Cargo Rail, France |
| 66218 | | Euro Cargo Rail, France |
| 66219 | | Euro Cargo Rail, France |
| 66220 | | DB Schenker Rail Polska, Poland |
| 66222 | | Euro Cargo Rail, France |
| 66223 | | Euro Cargo Rail, France |
| 66224 | | Euro Cargo Rail, France |
| 66225 | | Euro Cargo Rail, France |
| 66226 | | Euro Cargo Rail, France |
| 66227 | | DB Schenker Rail Polska, Poland |
| 66228 | | Euro Cargo Rail, France |
| 66229 | | Euro Cargo Rail, France |
| 66231 | | Euro Cargo Rail, France |
| 66233 | | Euro Cargo Rail, France |
| 66234 | | Euro Cargo Rail, France |
| 66235 | | Euro Cargo Rail, France |
| 66236 | | Euro Cargo Rail, France |
| 66237 | | DB Schenker Rail Polska, Poland |
| 66239 | | Euro Cargo Rail, France |
| 66240 | | Euro Cargo Rail, France |
| 66241 | | Euro Cargo Rail, France |
| 66242 | | Euro Cargo Rail, France |
| 66243 | | Euro Cargo Rail, France |
| 66244 | | Euro Cargo Rail, France |
| 66245 | | Euro Cargo Rail, France |
| 66246 | | Euro Cargo Rail, France |
| 66247 | | Euro Cargo Rail, France |
| 66248 | | DB Schenker Rail Polska, Poland |
| 66249 | | Euro Cargo Rail, France |
| 66411 | 66013 | Freightliner, Poland |
| 66412 | 66015 | Freightliner, Poland |
| 66417 | 66014 | Freightliner, Poland |
| 66582 | 66009 | Freightliner, Poland |
| 66583 | 66010 | Freightliner, Poland |
| 66584 | 66011 | Freightliner, Poland |
| 66586 | 66008 | Freightliner, Poland |
| 66608 | 66603 | Freightliner, Poland |
| 66609 | 66604 | Freightliner, Poland |
| 66611 | 66605 | Freightliner, Poland |
| 66612 | 66606 | Freightliner, Poland |
| 66624 | 66602 | Freightliner, Poland |
| 66625 | 66601 | Freightliner, Poland |

## Class 86

| | | |
|---|---|---|
| 86215 | 91 55 0450 005-8 | FLOYD, Hungary |
| 86217 | 91 55 0450 006-6 | FLOYD, Hungary |
| 86218 | 91 55 0450 004-1 | FLOYD, Hungary |
| 86228 | 91 55 0450 007-4 | FLOYD, Hungary |
| 86232 | 91 55 0450 003-3 | FLOYD, Hungary |
| 86233 | | Bulmarket, Bulgaria (S) |
| 86242 | 91 55 0450 008-2 | FLOYD, Hungary |
| 86248 | 91 55 0450 001-7 | FLOYD, Hungary |
| 86250 | 91 55 0450 002-5 | FLOYD, Hungary |
| 86424 | 91 55 0450 009-0 | FLOYD, Hungary (S) |

## Class 87

| | | |
|---|---|---|
| 87003 | 87003-0 | BZK, Bulgaria |
| 87004 | 87004-8 Britannia | BZK, Bulgaria |
| 87006 | 87006-3 | BZK, Bulgaria |
| 87007 | 87007-1 | BZK, Bulgaria |
| 87008 | 87008-9 | BZK, Bulgaria (S) |
| 87009 | | Bulmarket, Bulgaria |
| 87010 | 87010-5 | BZK, Bulgaria |
| 87012 | 87012-1 | BZK, Bulgaria |
| 87013 | 87013-9 | BZK, Bulgaria |
| 87014 | 87014-7 | BZK, Bulgaria (S) |
| 87017 | Iron Duke | Bulmarket, Bulgaria |
| 87019 | 87019-6 | BZK, Bulgaria |
| 87020 | 87020-4 | BZK, Bulgaria |
| 87022 | 87022-0 | BZK, Bulgaria |
| 87023 | Velocity | Bulmarket, Bulgaria |
| 87025 | | Bulmarket, Bulgaria |
| 87026 | 87026-1 | BZK, Bulgaria |
| 87028 | 87028-7 | BZK, Bulgaria |
| 87029 | 87029-5 | BZK, Bulgaria |
| 87033 | 87033-7 | BZK, Bulgaria |
| 87034 | 87034-5 | BZK, Bulgaria |

## Class 92

| | | |
|---|---|---|
| 92001 | 91 53 0472 002-1 Mircea Eliade | DB Schenker, Romania |
| 92002 | H.G. Wells | DB Schenker, Romania |
| 92005 | Mozart | DB Schenker, Romania |
| 92012 | 91 53 0472 001-3 Mihai Eminescu | DB Schenker, Romania |
| 92024 | J.S. Bach | DB Schenker, Romania |
| 92025 | Oscar Wilde | DB Schenker, Bulgaria |
| 92027 | George Eliot | DB Schenker, Bulgaria |
| 92030 | Ashford | DB Schenker, Bulgaria |
| 92034 | Kipling | DB Schenker, Bulgaria |
| 92039 | Johann Strauss | DB Schenker, Romania |

# 7. CODES

## 7.1. LIVERY CODES

Livery codes are used to denote the various liveries carried. It is impossible to list every livery variation which currently exists, in particular items ignored for this publication include:

* Minor colour variations.
* Omission of logos.
* All numbering, lettering and brandings.

Descriptions quoted are thus a general guide only. Logos as appropriate for each livery are normally deemed to be carried. The colour of the lower half of the bodyside is stated first.

| | |
|---|---|
| **1** | "One" (metallic grey with a broad black bodyside stripe. White National Express/Abellio Greater Anglia "interim" stripe as branding). |
| **AB** | Arriva Trains Wales/Welsh Government sponsored dark blue. |
| **AI** | Aggregate Industries (green, light grey & blue). |
| **AL** | Advertising/promotional livery (see class heading for details). |
| **AR** | Anglia Railways (turquoise blue with a white stripe). |
| **AZ** | Advenza Freight (deep blue with green Advenza brandings). |
| **B** | BR blue. |
| **BL** | BR Revised blue with yellow cabs, grey roof, large numbers & logo. |
| **CA** | Caledonian Sleeper (dark blue). |
| **CD** | Cotswold Rail (silver with blue & red logo). |
| **CE** | BR Civil Engineers (yellow & grey with black cab doors & window surrounds). |
| **CM** | Chiltern Mainline loco-hauled (two-tone grey & silver with blue stripes). |
| **CS** | Colas Rail (yellow, orange & black). |
| **CU** | Corus (silver with red logos). |
| **DB** | DB Schenker (Deutsche Bahn red with grey roof and solebar). |
| **DC** | Devon & Cornwall Railways (metallic silver). |
| **DG** | BR Departmental (dark grey with black cab doors & window surrounds). |
| **DI** | New DRS {Class 68 style} (deep blue & aquamarine with large compass logo). |
| **DR** | Direct Rail Services (dark blue with light blue or dark grey roof). |
| **DS** | Revised Direct Rail Services (dark blue, light blue & green. "Compass" logo). |
| **E** | English Welsh & Scottish Railway (maroon bodyside & roof with a broad gold bodyside band). |
| **EB** | Eurotunnel (two-tone grey with a broad blue stripe). |
| **EC** | East Coast (silver or grey with a purple stripe). |
| **ECR** | Euro Cargo Rail (light grey). |
| **EG** | "EWS grey" (as **F** but with large yellow & red EWS logo). |
| **EL** | Electric Traction Limited (silver & red). |
| **EP** | European Passenger Services (two-tone grey with dark blue roof). |
| **EX** | Europhoenix (silver, blue & red). |
| **F** | BR Trainload Freight (two-tone grey with black cab doors & window surrounds. Various logos). |

| FA | Fastline Freight (grey & black with white & orange stripes). |
|---|---|
| FB | First Group dark blue. |
| FE | Railfreight Distribution International (two tone-grey with black cab doors & dark blue roof). |
| FER | Fertis (light grey with a dark grey roof & solebar). |
| FF | Freightliner grey (two-tone grey with black cab doors & window surrounds. Freightliner logo). |
| FH | Revised Freightliner {PowerHaul} (dark green with yellow ends & a grey stripe/buffer beam). |
| FL | Freightliner (dark green with yellow cabs). |
| FO | BR Railfreight (grey bodysides, yellow cabs & red lower bodyside stripe, large BR logo). |
| FR | Fragonset Railways (black with silver roof & a red bodyside band lined out in white). |
| FS | First Group (indigo blue with pink & white stripes). |
| FY | Foster Yeoman (blue & silver. Cast numberplates). |
| G | BR Green (plain green, with white stripe on main line locomotives). |
| GA | Abellio Greater Anglia (white with a black stripe). |
| GB | GB Railfreight (blue with orange cantrail & solebar stripes, orange cabs). |
| GC | Grand Central (all over black with an orange stripe). |
| GG | BR green (two-tone green). |
| GIF | GIF (Spain) light blue with a dark blue band. |
| GL | First Great Western locomotives (green with a gold stripe (no gold stripe on shunters). |
| GW | Great Western Railway (TOC) dark green. |
| GY | Eurotunnel (grey & yellow). |
| HA | Hanson Quarry Products (dark blue/silver with oxide red roof). |
| HN | Harry Needle Railroad Company (orange with a black roof and solebar). |
| IC | BR InterCity (dark grey/white/red/white). |
| K | Black. |
| LH | BR Loadhaul (black with orange cabsides). |
| LM | London Midland (white/grey & green with broad black stripe around windows). |
| M | BR maroon. |
| ML | BR Mainline Freight (aircraft blue with a silver stripe). |
| N | BR Network SouthEast (white & blue with red lower bodyside stripe, grey solebar & cab ends). |
| NX | National Express (white with grey ends). |
| O | Non-standard (see class heading for details). |
| PC | Pullman Car Company (umber & cream with gold lettering lined out in gold). |
| RB | Riviera Trains Oxford blue. |
| RG | BR Parcels (dark grey & red). |
| RP | Royal Train (claret, lined out in red & black). |
| RR | Regional Railways (dark blue & grey with light blue & white stripes, three narrow dark blue stripes at vehicle ends). |
| RS | RMS Locotec blue. |
| RX | Rail Express Systems (dark grey & red with or without blue markings). |
| RZ | Royal Train revised (plain claret, no lining). |
| SD | South West Trains outer suburban {Class 450 style} (deep blue, orange & red). |
| SL | Silverlink (indigo blue with white stripe, green lower body & yellow doors). |

**SN** Southern (white & dark green with light green semi-circles at one end of each vehicle. Light grey band at solebar level).
**ST** Stagecoach (blue with red cabs).
**TT** Transmart Trains (all over green).
**U** White or grey undercoat.
**V** Virgin Trains (red with black doors extending into bodysides, three white lower bodyside stripes).
**VE** Virgin Trains East Coast (red & white with black window surrounds).
**VN** Belmond Northern Belle (crimson lake & cream lined out in gold).
**VP** Virgin Trains shunters (black with a large black & white chequered flag on the bodyside).
**WA** Wabtec Rail (black).
**WC** West Coast Railway Company maroon.
**XC** CrossCountry (two-tone silver with deep crimson ends and pink doors).
**Y** Network Rail yellow.

# 7.2. OWNER CODES

Locomotives and rolling stock are owned by various companies and private owners and are allotted codes as follows:

| | |
|---|---|
| 20 | Class 20189 |
| 40 | Class 40 Preservation Society |
| 47 | Stratford 47 Group |
| 50 | Class 50 Alliance |
| 56 | Class 56 Locomotives |
| 70 | 7029 Clun Castle |
| 71 | 71A Locomotives |
| 2L | Class Twenty Locomotives |
| A | Angel Trains |
| AI | Aggregate Industries |
| AM | Alstom |
| AV | Arriva UK Trains |
| BA | British American Railway Services |
| CS | Colas Rail |
| DB | DB Schenker Rail (UK) |
| DP | Deltic Preservation Society |
| DR | Direct Rail Services |
| DT | The Diesel Traction Group |
| E | Eversholt Rail (UK) |
| EL | Electric Traction Limited |
| EM | East Midlands Trains |
| EP | Europhoenix |
| ET | Eurotunnel |
| EU | Eurostar International |
| FG | First Group |
| FL | Freightliner |
| FW | Great Western Railway (assets of the Greater Western franchise) |
| GB | GB Railfreight |
| GV | Govia Thameslink Railway |
| HA | Hanson UK |

| | |
|---|---|
| HJ | Howard Johnston |
| HN | Harry Needle Railroad Company |
| LF | Lombard Finance |
| LM | London Midland |
| LS | Locomotive Services |
| MQ | Macquarie Group |
| MW | Martin Walker |
| NB | Neil Boden |
| NM | National Museum of Science & Industry |
| NR | Network Rail |
| NS | Nemesis Rail |
| NY | North Yorkshire Moors Railway Enterprises |
| P | Porterbrook Leasing Company |
| PC | Pamplona Capital Management |
| PP | Peter Pan Locomotive Company |
| RE | Railway Vehicle Engineering |
| RL | Rail Management Services (trading as RMS Locotec) |
| RV | Riviera Trains |
| TT | Transmart Trains |
| UR | UK Rail Leasing |
| WA | Wabtec Rail Group |
| WC | West Coast Railway Company |

# 7.3. LOCOMOTIVE POOL CODES

Locomotives are split into operational groups ("pools") for diagramming
and maintenance purposes. The official codes used to denote these pools
are shown in this publication.

| | |
|---|---|
| ACAC | Electric Traction Limited locomotives |
| ACXX | Electric Traction Limited locomotives for static depot use. |
| ATLO | Alstom Class 08. |
| AWCA | West Coast Railway Company operational locomotives. |
| AWCX | West Coast Railway Company stored locomotives. |
| CFOL | Class 50 Operations locomotives. |
| COFS | Colas Rail Classes 47 & 56. |
| COLO | Colas Rail Classes 47, 60, 66 & 70. |
| COLS | Colas Rail stored locomotives. |
| COTS | Colas Rail Class 37. |
| DFGH | Freightliner Heavy Haul Class 70. |
| DFGI | Freightliner Intermodal Class 70. |
| DFHG | Freightliner Heavy Haul low emission Class 66. |
| DFHH | Freightliner Heavy Haul Class 66. |
| DFIM | Freightliner Intermodal Class 66. |
| DFIN | Freightliner Intermodal low emission Class 66. |
| DFLC | Freightliner Intermodal Class 90. |
| DFLH | Freightliner Heavy Haul Class 47. |
| DFLS | Freightliner Class 08. |
| DFMC | Freightliner Intermodal Class 86/5. |
| DFNC | Freightliner Intermodal Class 86/6. |
| DHLT | Freightliner locomotives awaiting maintenance/repair/disposal. |

| | |
|---|---|
| EFOO | Great Western Railway Class 57. |
| EFPC | Great Western Railway 43. |
| EFSH | Great Western Railway 08. |
| EHPC | CrossCountry Class 43. |
| EJLO | London Midland Class 08. |
| ELRD | East Lancashire Railway-based main line registered locomotives. |
| EMPC | East Midlands Trains Class 43. |
| EMSL | East Midlands Trains Class 08. |
| EPEX | Europhoenix locomotives for export. |
| EPUK | Europhoenix UK locomotives. |
| ETLO | Electric Traction Limited Class 87. |
| GBCH | GB Railfreight Class 86 & 87. |
| GBCM | GB Railfreight Class 66. General. |
| GBCS | GB Railfreight Clas 73/9. Caledonian Sleeper. |
| GBDF | GB Railfreight Class 47. |
| GBDR | GB Railfreight Class 66. Locomotives from Germany. |
| GBED | GB Railfreight Class 73. |
| GBEE | GB Railfreight Class 20. On hire from Harry Needle/Class 20189. |
| GBET | GB Railfreight Class 92. Stored locomotives. |
| GBFM | GB Railfreight Class 66. RETB fitted. |
| GBNB | GB Railfreight Class 66. New build. |
| GBNL | GB Railfreight Class 66. Locomotives from the Netherlands. |
| GBNR | GB Railfreight Class 73/9. Network Rail contracts. |
| GBRT | GB Railfreight Class 66. Network Rail duties. |
| GBSD | GB Railfreight Class 66. |
| GBSL | GB Railfreight Class 92. Caledonian Sleeper. |
| GBST | GB Railfreight Class 92. Caledonian Sleeper & Channel Tunnel. |
| GBWM | GB Railfreight Class 08/09. |
| GBYH | GB Railfreight Class 59. |
| GCHP | Grand Central Class 43. |
| GPSS | Eurostar (UK) Class 08. |
| HBSH | Wabtec hire shunting locomotives. |
| HNRL | Harry Needle Railroad Company hire locomotives. |
| HNRS | Harry Needle Railroad Company stored locomotives. |
| HTLX | British American Railway Services locomotives. |
| HWSU | Govia Thameslink Railway Class 09. |
| HYWD | South West Trains Class 73. |
| IANA | Abellio Greater Anglia Class 90. |
| IECA | Virgin Trains East Coast Class 91. |
| IECP | Virgin Trains East Coast Class 43. |
| MBDL | Non TOC-owned diesel locomotives. |
| MBED | Non TOC-owned electro-diesel locomotives. |
| MBEL | Non TOC-owned electric locomotives. |
| MOLO | Class 20189 Ltd Class 20s. |
| MRSO | RMS Locotec Class 08. |
| NRLO | Nemesis Rail locomotives. |
| QADD | Network Rail diesel locomotives. |
| QCAR | Network Rail New Measurement Train Class 43. |
| QETS | Network Rail Class 37. |
| RFSH | Wabtec Rail locomotives. |
| RTLO | Riviera Trains Class 47. |

| | |
|---|---|
| RVLO | Rail Vehicle Engineering locomotives. |
| UKRL | UK Rail Leasing. Locomotives on lease. |
| UKRO | UK Rail Leasing. Locomotives for overhaul. |
| UKRS | UK Rail Leasing. Stored locosmotives. |
| WAAC | DB Schenker Class 67. |
| WABC | DB Schenker Class 67. RETB fitted. |
| WAWC | DB Schenker Class 67 for hire to Arriva Trains Wales. |
| WBAE | DB Schenker Class 66. Locomotives fitted with "stop-start" technology. |
| WBAT | DB Schenker Class 66. |
| WBBE | DB Schenker Class 66. RETB fitted and fitted with "stop-start" technology. |
| WBBT | DB Schenker Class 66. RETB fitted. |
| WBLE | DB Schenker Class 66. Dedicated locomotives for Lickey Incline banking duties. Fitted with "stop-start" technology. |
| WBLT | DB Schenker Class 66. Dedicated locomotives for Lickey Incline banking duties. |
| WBTT | DB Schenker Class 66. Fitted with tripcocks. |
| WCAT | DB Schenker Class 60. |
| WCBT | DB Schenker Class 60. Extended-range fuel tanks. |
| WDAM | DB Schenker Class 59. |
| WEAC | DB Schenker Class 90. |
| WEDC | DB Schenker Class 90 for hire to Caledonian Sleeper. |
| WFAC | DB Schenker Class 92. |
| WFBC | DB Schenker Class 92 with commissioned TVM430 cab signalling equipment for use on High Speed 1. |
| WGEE | DB Schenker Class 92 for export. |
| WQAA | DB Schenker stored locomotives Group 1A (short-term maintenance). |
| WQBA | DB Schenker stored locomotives Group 2 (unserviceable). |
| WQCA | DB Schenker stored locomotives Group 3 (unserviceable). |
| WQDA | DB Schenker stored locomotives Group 4 (awaiting disposal). |
| WSGC | DB Schenker Class 08/09. GSMR fitted. |
| WSRC | DB Schenker Class 08/09. Remote control fitted. |
| WSSC | DB Schenker Class 08/09. |
| XHAC | Direct Rail Services Classes 37/4, 47 & 57/3. |
| XHCE | Direct Rail Services Class 68 for hire to Chiltern Railways. |
| XHCK | Direct Rail Services Class 57/0. |
| XHHP | Direct Rail Services locomotives – holding pool. |
| XHIM | Direct Rail Services locomotives – Intermodal traffic. |
| XHNC | Direct Rail Services locomotives – nuclear traffic/general. |
| XHSS | Direct Rail Services stored locomotives. |
| XHVE | Direct Rail Services Class 68. |
| XHVT | Direct Rail Services Class 57/3 for hire to Virgin Trains West Coast. |
| XYPA | Mendip Rail Class 59/1. |
| XYPO | Mendip Rail Class 59/0. |

# 7.4. ALLOCATION & LOCATION CODES

Allocation codes are used in this publication to denote the normal maintenance base ("depots") of each operational locomotive. However, maintenance may be carried out at other locations and also by mobile teams. The designation (S) denotes stored.

| Code | Location | Depot Operator |
|------|----------|----------------|
| BA | Basford Hall Yard (Crewe) | Freightliner |
| BH | Barrow Hill (Chesterfield) | Barrow Hill Engine Shed Society |
| BL | Shackerstone, Battlefield Line | *Storage location only* |
| BM | Bournemouth | South West Trains |
| BN | Bounds Green (London) | Virgin Trains East Coast |
| BQ | Bury (Greater Manchester) | East Lancashire Rly Trust/Riley & Son (Railways) |
| BU | Burton-upon-Trent | Nemesis Rail |
| CE | Crewe International | DB Schenker Rail (UK) |
| CO | Coquelles (France) | Eurotunnel |
| CP | Crewe Arriva TrainCare | Arriva TrainCare |
| CR | Crewe Gresty Bridge | Direct Rail Services |
| CS | Carnforth | West Coast Railway Company |
| EC | Edinburgh Craigentinny | Virgin Trains East Coast |
| HT | Heaton (Newcastle) | Northern |
| KM | Carlisle Kingmoor | Direct Rail Services |
| KR | Kidderminster | Severn Valley Railway |
| LA | Laira (Plymouth) | Great Western Railway |
| LB | Loughborough Works | Wabtec Rail |
| LD | Leeds Midland Road | Freightliner Engineering |
| LE | Landore (Swansea) | Great Western Railway |
| LM | Long Marston (Warwickshire) | Quinton Rail Technology Centre |
| LR | Leicester | UK Rail Leasing |
| LT | Longport (Stoke-on-Trent) | Electro Motive Diesel Services |
| MD | Merehead | Mendip Rail |
| NC | Norwich Crown Point | Abellio Greater Anglia |
| NL | Neville Hill (Leeds) | East Midlands Trains/Northern |
| NY | Grosmont (North Yorkshire) | North Yorkshire Moors Railway Enterprises |
| OO | Old Oak Common HST | Great Western Railway |
| PG | Peterborough | GB Railfreight |
| RU | Rugby | Colas Rail |
| SE | St Leonards (Hastings) | St Leonards Railway Engineering |
| SH | Southall (London) | West Coast Railway Co/Locomotive Services |
| SL | Stewarts Lane (London) | Govia Thameslink Railway/Belmond |
| SK | Swanwick Junction (Derbyshire) | Midland Railway Enterprises |
| TM | Tyseley Locomotive Works | Birmingham Railway Museum |
| TO | Toton (Nottinghamshire) | DB Schenker Rail (UK) |
| WH | Washwood Heath (Birmingham) | Boden Rail Engineering/RMS Locotec |
| WN | Willesden (London) | London Overground |
| WO | Wolsingham, Weardale Railway | RMS Locotec |
| YK | National Railway Museum (York) | National Museum of Science & Industry |
| ZA | RTC Business Park (Derby) | Railway Vehicle Engineering |
| ZB | Doncaster Works | Wabtec Rail |
| ZC | Crewe Works | Bombardier Transportation UK |
| ZD | Derby Works | Bombardier Transportation UK |
| ZG | Eastleigh Works | Arlington Fleet Services |
| ZH | Springburn Depot (Glasgow) | Knorr-Bremse Rail Systems (UK) |
| ZI | Ilford Works | Bombardier Transportation UK |
| ZJ | Stoke-on-Trent Works | Axiom Rail (Stoke) |
| ZK | Kilmarnock Works | Wabtec Rail Scotland |
| ZN | Wolverton Works | Knorr-Bremse Rail Systems (UK) |
| ZR | York (Holgate Works) | Network Rail |